POLAND

EAST
GERMANY

CZEC   'A

HAFFENBURG

BAMBERG

NUREMBURG

REGENSBERG   METTEN

STRAUBING

PASSAU   OBERZELL   DÜRNSTEIN   KORNEUBERG

SCHLOGEN   GREIN

BAVARIA   LINZ   MELK   VIENNA

MAUTHAUSEN   YBBS

LOWER AUSTRIA   River Danube

ALPS   TYROL   AUSTRIA

UPPER AUSTRIA

ITALY   YUGOSLAVIA

D0955805

Leontyne

LEONTYNE

By barge from London to Vienna

RICHARD GOODWIN

COLLINS
8 Grafton Street, London W1
1989

William Collins Sons and Co. Ltd
London · Glasgow · Sydney · Auckland
Toronto · Johannesburg

BRITISH LIBRARY CATALOGUING IN PUBLICATION DATA
Goodwin, Richard
Leontyne: by barge from London to Vienna.
1. Europe. Inland waterways. Description & travel
I. Title
914'.04558

ISBN 0-00-215390-4

This book accompanies the television programmes
produced by Leontyne Films Ltd
for Central Independent Television plc

Photoset in Linotron Palatino by
Rowland Phototypesetting Ltd
Bury St Edmunds, Suffolk

Printed in Great Britain by
William Collins Sons & Co. Ltd, Glasgow

To my wife

Contents

List of Illustrations

(All photographs copyright Central Independent Television plc
except where indicated otherwise.)

Acknowledgements

I should like to acknowledge the enormous amount of help which I received during the course of my voyage from all those who went out of their way to be of assistance and to make the journey possible. I wish to make special mention of help received from Marion Swaybill of WNET, New York, Richard Creasey and Roger James of Central Independent Television and John Brabourne, partner and friend.

Leontyne and I

I can't remember when my dream turned into a plan, but I do remember when real things started to happen. I remember standing on the Pont des Arts in Paris one morning and watching the barges ploughing up and down. They were complete; families, children, even a car on board for some. Where they stopped for the night was home, wherever they were. It was then I decided that I wanted to sample the half-gypsy life that these people lead; stopping, making new friends here and there and, above all, greeting the bright morning light over the countryside, always changing, always new.

I live by the river in London, so some years back I put out some inquiries amongst the river people I knew and, to my surprise, within days I was told they had just what I wanted, a converted launch tug. A bit too soon, I thought, but I went to have a look all the same. There she was, black and rusty and cruelly converted into a kind of cabin cruiser. The motor was far too small for such a heavy boat, the hull was thin in places and in many parts there was a layer of concrete to stop leaks. But there was something about her tenacious shape and lowness in the water that made me feel that she could carry me to wherever I wanted in perfect safety. Her vital statistics were 30 feet long, 9 feet wide and she drew just on 4 feet of water. She weighed over 14 tons and was so low in the water that she could pass under almost any bridge. A deal was struck, probably too much, but for £4000 she was mine.

I had to register her name with the relevant authorities

13

before I could go anywhere, in this case with the Board of Trade. This vessel of mine was known to all who worked on the Thames as the *Leo*. I liked the name but the Registry said that there were nine other Leos and if mine was to be the tenth, I would have to produce her birth certificate. This proved to be impossible. The best I could do was to find out that she had been built in 1926. By whom and where was very unclear. Some said Odell's Yard at Brentford: some misty eyes remembered Odell bringing her over from Holland to use as a template for other similar tugs he was building. As I delved, I found out that the *Leo* had been owned by all sorts of river people, some of whom had passed bundles of notes to each other and were guarded about their ownership in any case: they certainly didn't have any bits of paper. One of these likely lads, a gloomy ex-lighterman, volunteered that I would certainly perish in her, as he had nearly done going round to Harwich when a sudden storm blew up.

Alarmed, I went down to the berth where she was lying and had a serious moment wondering whether this was a final madness. But I knew in my heart that I would never be happy if I didn't get to France; so all possible risks were forgotten and the preparations began. I had registered the boat as the *Leontyne* but by all her friends she is still known as the *Leo*, strange hermaphroditic beast that she is. The wondrous sound of Leontyne Price's voice (on my very first visit to the opera, I heard her sing *Aida* in Milan) could well also have had something to do with my choice of name.

Before the great adventure described in this book, I took the *Leo* on several voyages, preparations, as it turned out, for the big one. Our first Channel crossing was uneventful until we were in the middle of the main shipping lane. We were using the proper procedure to cross at right angles so as to be in the danger zone for as little time as possible, when quite suddenly, one of the rigid fuel lines on the engine burst. Something like that happens very rarely. Fortunately we had a spare but fitting it as we rolled about in the wash of half a million tons of supertanker was alarming. At last, one of my friends from the river, Paul Wilson, finished the job and the engine turned over again. I wondered if we had made even the tiniest blob on anybody's radar.

I took my family through Paris and round the glorious canals in the centre of France and then decided that I should have to bring the *Leo* home and put a bigger engine in her. After two years of wandering through the summers I recrossed the Channel and had a new engine put in for the next expedition.

This voyage was from London to Calais with one foot in the gutter, as it were, round to Cherbourg, and then down to St Malo. We only just made it before the weather broke, after five clear calm days in May. Then, on through the Brittany Canals, which are too narrow for today's commercial traffic, to Redon and then to Nantes and out into the Bay of Biscay.

We had to turn back almost at once, as the huge Atlantic swells got hold of the *Leo* and tossed her about like a plastic cup. Chastened, we ran for cover to St Nazaire. Happy to limp into harbour we spent the night in the old submarine pens, a night that will be long remembered by the ship's company, my children, Sabine and Jason. Cold, uncomfortable and noisy; the fishing fleet tied up and unloaded their fish next to us just when we had nodded off. Still it was a great deal better than some watery grave off the Isle of Noirmoutier.

The next year I continued through the Bay of Biscay in perfect weather and up the Gironde to Bordeaux. Then I set out through some of the most beautiful parts of France. I remember eating fritters made from the flowers of acacia that a lady lock-keeper, seeing I was alone, had kindly made for my supper. In these parts, the lock-keepers have sovereign rights, it seems, over the land fifty yards up- and downstream of their lock. I had asked to moor in the shade under the enormous acacia trees, and that was how I came to eat this

15

delicious and recherché meal. I gave her a plastic bottle of Scotch whisky for her husband. As I left in the dawn the éclusière, rather shyly I thought, gave me half a dozen eggs. She said that she was very grateful for the Scotch and indicated that her husband had enjoyed it and her. I suppose May is rather a good time for that sort of thing.

As the Leo and I ploughed our way through the peaceful canals lined with yellow wild irises, the water covered with the fluffy flowers of the acacia trees that lined the bank, it came to me that here was real exploration. Discovery of what life could be like if lived at a human pace. Just the odd contact every hour or so with a lock-keeper and time to think without fear of interruption. I began to think about where else I could go after I had completed my present trip, how it could be financed and whether I really wanted to do it. Perhaps I was seduced by the idyllic surroundings, but it was here I decided that I would make a real voyage, not just a holiday adventure, to some faraway place. If I could get it together, I would try to go down the Rhine, up the Main, over the European watershed (the watershed stretch would have to be by land as the new canal currently in construction would not be finished for some years) and then down the Danube to Vienna. Of course the Leo would not have enough accommodation for a lengthy trip but perhaps since she was a tug she could tow a barge or even, as was becoming more fashionable, push one.

After my couple of trips abroad, I felt I was ready for the big voyage. The Leo and I had done our homework. I knew what she needed and knew where we were going. The only thing that remained was to finance the adventure. Now, I've worked in movies all my life, doing a bit of everything, and, if there is one thing I've learned, it is that if you really want to do anything, you have to make a serious start yourself with whatever resources you have available. It seems that personal commitment and enthusiasm are the main ingredients for persuading financiers of the worth of a project. So I decided to convert over the next year the *Mercat*, a Thames lighter that at one time had been a high-security barge, which meant, amongst other things, that it had a galvanized hull. The first major work was to take out the ceiling of the barge (oddly named as it is in fact the floor). The boards had completely rotted and we had to replace them with a special mixture of fast-drying concrete up to the level of the steel frames of the hull – about nine inches of concrete were required. Quick-drying concrete has to be used because the mixture must dry while the vessel in on a flat bottom – if the tide comes in before the concrete is properly set it will dry at an angle, meaning your boat has a permanent list.

Then the ordering began, and all that winter welders worked intermittently, installing all the big items, in the correct order. Holes were cut in the aft deck for the generator which was housed behind the aft bulkhead. Steel box bars were rolled to form the same curves as the combings, so that the hold of the barge was enclosed. Doors were cut in the bulkheads and tanks were installed for water and fuel.

Once the welding was out of the way, the carpenters got cracking. I installed a formidable diesel cooker which I found in a chandler's who had had it in his basement for eight years (meaning that I got it cheap). There were three sleeping cabins, one which I had designed for my daughter Sabine, a double one for guests, and my cabin, which was naturally slightly larger than the others with a desk in it, as I had visions of writing Captain Bligh-type logs far into the night. In the event I was nearly always too exhausted to do anything but jump into bed and fall asleep.

The total area on the barge available for living was sixteen by thirty-three feet. Apart from the cabins, there were two bathrooms, both with electric lavatories which always blocked at the most inopportune moments. The forward bathroom had a minuscule bath which was hardly ever used on the voyage, not because we were particularly dirty people but because it was such a performance to have a bath and

17

we frequently did not have enough water. We had to make other arrangements. The rest of the area was made up of the saloon, which was lined on the port side with the diesel cooker – this also coped with the central heating – a double sink and a freezer. In the middle, I had put a table from a monastery that I had bought years before in the New Forest. In the swinheads, the angled bits at the ends of the barge, I had fitted a generator in the aft section and in the larger forward section there was a 400-gallon fresh-water tank, a holding tank for the sewage, and a massive bank of batteries to give us a 24-volt DC supply plus a back-up bank in case they failed.

Entrance to the barge was from the stern of the saloon down a stairway, under which was a hot water tank which was heated by both the central heating and the generator. This very nearly caused an accident on one occasion when we left the generator running with no water in the system: the effect was rather like the invention of the steam engine and caused a considerable explosion, splitting the sides of the copper canister as though it were a rotten peach. The interior of the barge was lit by ports in the deck above and by portholes in the sloping sides of the barge which reflected dancing light off the water in a most pleasing manner.

All through the early summer months, I tried out the rig. The *Leo* was now pushing the barge which I had renamed the *Leontine* to make the lock-keepers believe that it was really the same vessel and thus reduce the paperwork – a ruse that I am happy to say worked very well. Because of the huge pressures on the deck equipment we had a number of breakages. Pins snapped off, steel wires broke and it became obvious that this was an area that I simply could not afford to try to save money on. So I had to exchange all the winches holding the two boats together for heavier gear. Up and down the Thames we went, raising eyebrows everywhere. Over and over again I was told that I couldn't think of getting to Vienna in that.

At the end of June I decided that I must try out the new towing post. Pushing the barge up river to Putney, the gearbox overheated and we had to stop to let it cool down. On the way back to Rotherhithe I decided to tow the barge, which I thought would be better for the gearbox and perhaps not give it quite so much work to do. As we went downstream the ebb tide got stronger and stronger and I began to realize that I wasn't going to be able to stop very easily. As we raced under London Bridge and then Tower Bridge, the spring ebb tide was at its full force. I was alone on the tug, with the rest of the crew, which included Sabine, on the barge; there was no means of communication with them as they were below decks. I started to get really alarmed.

To stop in these circumstances meant that I would have to chuck round, that is to say that I would have to bring the tug, with the barge following, round into the current at just the right moment or I would be swept past the mooring I wanted to go to; this, in turn, was drying out so fast as the tide went out that soon there would be no water for us to come alongside. I tried the manoeuvre. As the *Leo* came round to face the tide, the engine and gearbox failed to give me the punch I needed. The barge and the *Leo* jack-knifed, the towrope trapped me against the steering wheel and then I felt the whole weight of the barge, all forty-two tons, press against my abdomen. I was literally squashed, but the rope slackened for a moment, giving me just enough time to haul my semi-paralysed lower half up on to the barge. As I did so, the bow of the barge crashed through the wheelhouse of the *Leo*, a blow which would have done for me if I had been in the way. I lay on the deck not able to move or do much at all, except to admire Sabine's courage as she leapt from the barge on to the tug, and tried to correct our course. Miraculously, a police launch happened to be passing, finding us careering helplessly down the Thames on a five-knot tide. They took some time, it seemed to me, to assess the situation; in the meantime Sabine managed to steer the tug in approximately the right direction, making to throw a line to the police boat. At this point I blacked out.

Further events are somewhat hazy, except that I remember my dear wife leaning over me as I promised her I would sell the boats and live a calmer life.

CHAPTER ONE

London to Calais

I was out of action for six weeks and as I lay in my hospital bed overlooking the Pool of London, I watched the hordes of office workers streaming to and fro over London Bridge. The new 'London Bridge City' is quite a sight at dawn, but, when the sun comes up, its concrete canyons are, alas, just the same as any other project which has been built for the continuing glory of its architects, rather than the poor souls who have to struggle round its windswept gulches. What are they all dreaming about – making their fortunes from the VDU screen? Or perhaps making their escape? What do people dream of today? Once the movies provided dreams of romance and luxury, but today everyone knows the plot. Violence, more violence and sex is all that is being provided, by and large. I dreamed of quiet places with calm water, bread, cheese and a bottle of wine, and above all I dreamed of being in control of my destiny for a time, amongst the rivers of Europe. Perhaps I would be able to persuade someone to back me in what would seem to many a dotty venture.

It was obvious to me by now that I would need professional help in the adventure to improve the odds on completing the journey more or less unscathed. Ray Julian was one of the elite band of Thames watermen who had spent seven years as an apprentice before getting his papers as a licensed waterman. These years of learning are very important on the Thames, a savage and unpredictable river as I knew to my cost. Over the journey, I realized what an enormously resilient person he was. There was hardly ever a situation that he had not experienced when it came to handling boats and he had the true professional attitude to electrical and mechanical machinery which, if he did not understand how to mend, he would find someone who really did. He kept himself amazingly fit by going for long runs along the towpath at dawn every morning and eating masses of honey with everything. He had two grown-up sons and a very pretty daughter. I had run into him through my contacts on the river and had liked him as soon as I met him as he was clearly a gypsy at heart like me and we got on at once. By the end of the trip, I had the greatest respect for him and his appreciation of the natural beauty through which we travelled, which was far more intense than many an Oxbridge mind I have encountered. My journey would have been a lot more difficult and far less fun without his good humour and stamina.

At the beginning of September 1987, I was well enough to start trials again and get the *Leo*'s rig correctly fixed. The biggest problem was the lack of sufficient power. The best and cheapest remedy seemed to be a bigger propeller, but a bigger propeller meant a stronger gearbox; this, in turn, meant a more powerful engine, and that I couldn't possibly afford. In the end I decided not to waste any more time, but to concentrate instead on raising the finance for the voyage which would also have to cover the cost of the six-cylinder Gardner engine that I was planning to get, reconditioned, from a London bus.

During the winter months, many little things were being finished off on the barge and I was slowly getting the boats into a condition which, if not exactly shipshape, might be described as working. The hydraulic steering on the boat had sprung a leak and we were at one time drifting without steering under Tower Bridge. Fundamental mechanical problems like this had dogged our progress, but that is often the way with dress rehearsals for a successful show.

At last, after a winter of biting my fingernails, the money

was raised from a British television company, Central Television, and now all that had to be done was to fix a date for our departure.

Our first night on board, in April 1988, was not without mishap. Ray was not yet with me, and, until he could join me, I had taken the services of another waterman, Reggie, a man with a huge and apparently random knowledge of geographical place names. As he moored us up, at Fisher's Wharf by London Bridge, and tied our warps round a pillar, he reeled off the names of the big towns on the Don and the Volga. 'No problem,' said he. 'When the tide goes down, just check the ropes, and all will be well. I bet you can't tell me what the Russian port at the mouth of the Danube is called.'

All was well on the descent, a fall of about eighteen feet, and I sank gratefully into bed, forgetting that in tidal terms what goes down must come up. I awoke, about 3.00 a.m., to find that for some reason the porthole in my cabin was covered with water, and I was falling to the bottom of my bed. I soon discovered that the warps had stuck on the pillar and that the barge was being held under as the tide rose swiftly around us. I rushed for the carving knife which, in those days, was still razor sharp. I had only to touch the blade against the bar-tight rope for the whole forty-odd tons of barge to shake itself free and bob up again from its undignified posture. Rattled, I returned to bed, realizing that for all the charm of Reggie's randomly acquired geographical trivia, I could rely on no one but myself for the safety of the boats.

The next evening we slipped down to the Thames Barrier and tied up next to the *Sir Aubrey*, a large river-tug, which had been built when the river was busier for towing long strings of barges. I talked to Ron Sargeant, the doyen of a famous waterman family on that part of the river. His forebears had built up their business a century or so before by rowing down to the mouth of the river, sometimes even as far as the Goodwin Sands, and throwing their grappling hooks on to ships bound for the Thames in order to get the pilotage before anyone else. His grandfather had been present at the disaster of the *Princess Alice*: a passenger boat full of Victorian families having a day out on the river collided with a small collier on a perfect summer's afternoon. Many people were drowned, and those who were not choked to death on the effluent that came streaming out from London's sewers just there. (To this day the largest tributary of the Thames is the treated sewage outlet a little further down the river.) Amongst the victims of this catastrophe had been the owners of the Crown and Anchor at Charlton. Ron Sargeant's grandfather had bought the pub at once and from then on the Sargeants had become the most powerful family on that part of the river.

We also spent a jolly day at Tower Bridge with the Keeper, Colonel Dalton, who, quoting V. S. Pritchett, called the bridge 'a purple passage suitable for the archers at Agincourt'. The origin of the V-sign lay apparently in the fact that the French, when they captured English bowmen, would chop off the index finger on their right hand so that they could not draw a bowstring properly. To frighten the enemy, the English archers would hold up both fingers showing that they were whole. I discovered that the walkway at the top of the bridge between the bascules had been insisted upon by the City Fathers, so that the public would not have to wait to cross while it was opened for passing ships. The bridgemen became very speedy at opening the bridge, however, and nobody could be bothered to climb the stairs and cross over the walkway. Before long it had become a gathering place for ladies of the night and had to be closed. Colonel Dalton also told me that the bridge's granite stones are merely cosmetic, there to hide the steelwork and make it resemble the Tower of London.

Tower Bridge, like Blackfriars, Southwark, and London, is owned by the Bridges Trust, a City of London foundation. On the Thames, London Bridge is known simply as 'The Bridge', probably dating back to the time when it was the only bridge, and also because it is the point where all the tidal predictions are made for the river traffic. Blackfriars Bridge is supposed to mark the upper reach of the salt water in the Thames. Sea-water birds are carved on the down-river side and fresh-water fowl on the upper. How many bridge builders would have the time, patience or wit to do that in these days?

On some days we seemed fated to meet lugubrious people. One was a river policeman who chatted for hours about the unfortunates whose bodies he had discovered in the Thames. The tide and the cold were the killers now, no longer the pollution. I suppose it is a *métier* like everything else, but on such a beautiful sunny morning it seemed strange to hear about the improvements he was trying for body recovery. Apparently it takes about three weeks for the gases to build up in the submerged corpse, which shoot it to the surface, by which time, he said, the limbs were becoming 'a little loose'. Men and women, contradicting each other to the end, float in opposite ways.

In the afternoon, I chatted to a gentleman from Trinity House, whose job it is to service the buoys and lighthouses round the coast of Britain. As we were talking he produced a flat piece of lead from his desk drawer. 'A replica of the lead found in the stomach of the keeper of the Eddystone Rock Lighthouse,' he said. It seems that this unfortunate lighthouse-keeper was standing on the rocks just below his lighthouse, which was burning fiercely. Looking up aghast, his mouth quite naturally fell open and in dropped the molten lead. Being a tough old boy he rowed ashore and told his unlikely tale which no one believed, but when he died three days later, an autopsy proved his story and the retrieved lead even contained imprints of the carrots he had eaten for his last meal. Apparently lighthouse-keepers became excellent cooks. It's too bad that all the lighthouses are being replaced by radar beacons. Someone has yet to introduce me to the romance of electronics.

The night of 13 April was my last night at home. The next day I was to take the noon tide to Erith where I would meet up with Ray. The *Leo* came alongside Grices Wharf in Rotherhithe, where I live, to take on final provisions, and I said farewell to Reggie. In the morning, I was given a pennant on which was embroidered a lion rampant (representing Leo), which made a proud sight fluttering in the breeze. All the people in the buildings came to give me a rousing send-off. Balloons, streamers, the lot. Captain Christopher Jones had set off from this very spot to collect the Pilgrim Fathers from Plymouth Sound on their historic journey. I bet he didn't get balloons or streamers. I certainly had a lump in my throat, but the moisture in the eye could well have been due to the biting north-easterly wind. Nautical departures have a strange effect on people. The sadness of leaving is almost immediately replaced by an intense excitement that will surely end with the voyage. My mother used to tell me how interesting eye-to-eye relationships would develop on the P&O ships going to India, even before England had disappeared over the horizon. By the Eddystone Rock the pairings were almost complete.

Through the Barrier for the last time. 'Are you inward- or outward-bound, sir?' the calm voice of the controller inquired. Outward-bound is what we were. Plump and fifty, I was leaving behind a life of pampering the pampered and never having to worry about the washing, never mind the washing-up. From now on, it was to be do it yourself. No more limos and lunches or gossip and gush. The 6.00 a.m. shipping forecast would replace the 'London Last Night' column or *Variety*'s latest roundup of box-office figures.

*

I decided that for our first night I would make fast on the buoy at Erith, which is a flat and desolate part of the Thames. I made a real hash of it as I thought that the tide had turned and was coming in, but to my surprise it was still going out (there is a back eddy just there as every waterman knows!). The result was that I shot past the buoy and had to make a ponderous turn to come in again in the right direction. Next morning, early, I took the dinghy and picked up Ray as arranged, from the bottom of the causeway that stretches out over the mudflats at Erith.

We set off for Gravesend, so called because after Gravesend all bodies were buried at sea. Some say that this was where the bodies from the Great Plague of London were buried but, logistically, that seems too fanciful to me. The tide soon started to run strongly against us and my confidence in the power of our excellent Gardner engine was a mite diminished. We pushed our way on through the stream and finally tied up on a buoy outside Custom House Pier, amongst the big seagoing tugs. Opposite, on Tilbury Pier, lay the new P&O palace, the *Sovereign of the Seas*. I'm afraid nobody is ever again destined to go by P&O to the land of the cake Parsee. No more fancy dress parties on the penultimate night before arriving in Bombay, when some joker would always come dressed as a baby and another would arrive with a lavatory seat around his neck to be the life and soul of the party. The Queen of Sheba and Nefertiti were, as I recall, favourites amongst the ladies. This elegant ship, however, had been built for the blue-rinse set off Honolulu.

First thing in the morning we set off, towing the barge to the Medway: we had decided to tow rather than push where there was the chance of getting any sizable waves. As it happened it was a glorious, though misty, morning with a promise of sun later. The air echoed with the mournful calling of the foghorns and we were very excited by the strange beauty of the shipping in the slight morning mist, and of the

27

chimneys burning off the waste petroleum gases at Shellhaven.

The first landmark to appear on the horizon was the wreck of the *Montgomery* – an American ammunition ship that went aground in the war and sank. It would be too dangerous to blow it up because apparently, even now, the explosion would shatter all the windows in Southend – some fifteen miles away. It made a melancholy sight with just the masts sticking out of the water and the moan of the marker buoy whistling as it bobbed about in the swell.

After a couple of hours, and almost out of sight of land, we came upon a fishing boat trawling for Dover sole. We stopped and for ten pounds we bought three splendid fish. It was hard to tell what they weighed because they stubbornly refused to lie still in the scales. Later, I fried them so hard that I set off the smoke alarm, but they were quite delicious.

That night we moored at Thunderbolt Pier, Chatham, quite a privilege for a ramshackle craft like ours. A few years earlier, whilst the Navy was there, only the most gleaming burnished pinnacles would have been allowed to touch the hallowed jetty. Now the Chatham Dockyards, where the *Fighting Temeraire* and the *Victory* had been built, had become a 'living museum'. At least the great buildings have been preserved but my feeling is that the once proud place is sinking inexorably into the land of the wicker basket.

I wandered round the ropery, through the yarn-combing and twisting areas, and then down to the main room where the rope is made. This is 220 metres long – 120 fathoms – long enough to make a coil of rope for the Royal Navy, which they have been doing since the end of the eighteenth century. I chatted to the men on the trolley that rolls up and down this long room, twisting the yarn into rope. They talked of better days, of ghosts, and the fact that most of the rope they were making went to Dartmoor prison for the inmates to make doormats with.

The best hemp comes from Riga in Russia and I decided to buy a length. I thought that Ray would be delighted, but when I presented it he turned up his nose and said hemp was dreadful stuff when it got wet. Perhaps that is what the rest of the boating fraternity say, which would explain why this place is a living museum: everyone now uses ropes made from man-made fibres. Even so, all through the centuries, through hot wars and cold wars, hemp has been finding its way from Riga to Chatham. I am always fascinated by the way that traders manage to rise above politics and continue to trade, in spite of the most enormous national upheavals. Pongees, of Clerkenwell Road in London, continued to get their silks from China right through the Cultural Revolution, and the Long March meant nothing to the tea markets.

I went to the Flag Loft, a pleasant place boasting lots of faded colour pictures of the Queen with her crown on, and resounding to the modern equivalent of *Workers Playtime* – the *Jimmy Young Show*, I suppose. They don't make White Ensigns any more, just house flags for office buildings. I wanted to buy a Rumanian courtesy flag, not that it would get me very far in that benighted country. A charming young girl said she would make the flags we needed within the hour but that she couldn't manage Rumania because it had a complicated crest in the middle, and no one went there anyway.

We left in the early afternoon and made our way to Queensborough at the mouth of the Swale, a river which runs from the Medway to Whitstable and is a sheltered passage for craft like ours. We had been having quite serious vibrations in the area of our propeller and wanted to have a look at the bottom of the *Leo* before we reached France. There would be no tide in the canals and that meant we would have to get the *Leo* lifted out by crane, whereas in Queensborough the tide would do it for us for nothing.

We found a pontoon, moored up the barge, ran the *Leo*

ashore, dropped two anchors, and waited for the tide to go out. When it did, it revealed that one of the two fins that I had welded on to the rudder some time back, in order to improve the steerage, had come off completely and the other had vibrated so much that it was hanging on by a whisker. The vibration was caused by a slightly loose rudder post and the huge turbulence of the water. With difficulty, we managed to get the portable generator to work and I ground the metal at the joint of the remaining fin until, after a little effort, it came away. Satisfied that we had done what we could we returned to the barge to have some supper, and wait for the tide to come in again. I decided that I should go and collect the *Leo* when the tide was right, at about 2.00 a.m., by which time she would be afloat.

When my alarm went off, I went up on deck and turned on the searchlight, swinging it this way and that, but to my consternation the *Leo* had completely disappeared. Really alarmed by now, I called Ray and we jumped into the dinghy. The outboard wouldn't start, which is the way with all outboards. As I struggled with the motor, I thought what a terrible mess it would be if I had really lost the *Leo*. At last the motor fired. I stood in the bows of the dinghy anxiously sweeping the horizon with a flashlight for a sign of our stubby little mast amongst the swaying masts and halyards of the yachts. Suddenly, at the very end of a row of boats, I saw the *Leo*. As the water had risen, she must have dragged her anchor and floated on the tide with her anchors trailing below her. When she reached the trots, the submerged chains to which the boats were moored, the anchors must have caught, and as long as the tide continued to flood, she would have been held in this position. As we came alongside and started to free the anchors, I looked over my shoulder and saw to my horror that we had drifted into the middle of the very narrow channel and that a huge sandboat was rushing up towards us. I leapt into the cabin, switching on all the navigation lights and the engine at the same moment. We've had

it, I thought, unless we get out of the way very sharply
indeed: there was no possibility that the approaching monster, towering sixty feet above us, ablaze with lights and
weighing at least ten thousand tons, would ever have been
able to stop. Mercifully the engine fired and we shot out of
the way, our anchors dragging on the bottom. With the
sandboat past, we crept thankfully back to the barge and to
bed.

We set out for Oare Creek, at the other end of the Swale
River from where we were lying. I wanted to call there to see
what the creeks round the Thames Estuary must have been
like in the old days, when there were smugglers and excise
men abroad. A special kind of Thames boot was invented by
the smugglers, with a kind of snow-shoe or tennis-racquet
shape strapped to its sole, so that the wearer didn't sink into
the mud. Smuggling brandy for the parson and baccy for
the clerk somehow seemed a good deal more romantic and
socially acceptable than lugging a cardboard suitcase with a
false bottom full of drugs through one of our lovelier airports.

We slipped down the Swale, which flows through lovely
unspoiled marshes, until we passed a small blue launch
which was just packing up its gear after taking some samples
of water for pollution checks. As we passed they set off, and
as soon as their backs were turned the waste pipe of an
enormous factory started vomiting out a dark purplish liquid.

Oare Creek is a small tributary of Faversham Creek and at
its junction, next to the Shipwright's Arms, the only other
building for miles around, Laurie Tester and Don Grover
have a wonderful, ramshackle boatyard. Laurie was brought
up in the family that owned the Greenhithe Lighterage
Company. It went out of business when the docks on the
Thames closed, but Laurie, who had already purchased the
land at Oare Creek, bought a tug from the liquidator and
went into business with Don Grover. Laurie is very particular

about describing the place as a boatyard rather than as a marina. Marinas, he said, were full of men in white overalls, and the expense of these gentlemen would have put Tom, Dick and Harry off from bringing their boats to him at Oare Creek.

Laurie and Don have a passion for racing Thames sailing barges round the Thames Estuary in the summer months. They skipper one each, and theirs is a deadly rivalry which in the past has caused broken bowsprits, so close do they steer to each other when rounding a buoy. I spent many hours chatting to them. As they told of storms and close shaves, with the precision of men who have really been there, they were both privately occupied in planning how they could best each other in the summer races round the estuary – a contest where only experience counts.

Laurie and Don promised to escort us on the tide to Whitstable the next day. I was getting very fearful about towing the barge in any kind of sea. The barge itself was fine, but the tug, *Leo*, was low in the water. She was very buoyant, and on her own could manage seas up to force five without much difficulty, but when she was towing the barge, she laboured a good deal in the slightest swell. I thought that with the expertise of Ray, who was, God bless him, game for anything, and with these two old salts in another tug, I should be able to get a pretty objective view of our chances of making the crossing to Calais.

We left soon after noon, down Faversham Creek into the Swale. It was the best kind of spring day, with beautiful clear air and a smart little breeze. Ray and I were so busy watching the towrope that we ran aground on a spit of sand when we got into the Swale. It wasn't a serious blunder and we were able to stumble off it in a few minutes, but we both felt very embarrassed under the unflappable gaze of Laurie and Don, who had correctly assessed us as amiable but inexperienced in the estuary. In an hour we arrived at Whitstable Harbour, which has a tricky entrance. With the wind blowing against the tide, we were quite seriously tossed about and were very glad when we got into the harbour, which isn't normally available to anything but small coasters, sandboats and fishing boats.

My plan was that we should spend a day or two here, make our final preparations for the Channel crossing, and wait for the weather: if it turned on us, we could always slip into Ramsgate and wait for a better day – or so I thought. On our first day in harbour the sea was, as the French so neatly put it, 'mer belle'. There was not a ripple in sight, and I decided that we should leave on the tide at 4.30 a.m. the next morning. My decision was also prompted by the knowledge that the sandboat whose berth we were occupying was due back on the morning tide.

We had a rendezvous with Laurie and Don in their tug, the *Evelyn Sperring*, at a buoy about three miles out in the estuary, from where they planned to escort us to Ramsgate. If the weather was good, I secretly hoped that we could make the crossing in our little boat in one hop. In the darkness, Ray and I prepared the tow and cheerfully set out, passing the incoming sandboat in the harbour entrance whose crew shouted down that the sea was as smooth as glass, just as the weathermen had predicted.

We had taken the precaution of buying some drainstoppers from the local civil engineering contractor, which we had placed in the portholes to prevent the wash from large ships from shattering the glass in the ports: a wise precaution as it turned out, for we were no more than twenty minutes out when a squall blew up and all the bonhomie of our departure evaporated as seas broke over the stern and soaked us to the skin. Head up into the wind, our problem now was how to turn back. Ray decided that the best thing to do was to lengthen the tow and come round while the rope was slack. With the water breaking over the stern of the *Leo* in great black lumps and pouring down into the cabin through the open door, this manoeuvre turned out to be a good deal more

33

hazardous than I could possibly have imagined. As Ray clung on to the wheel and ducked under the flailing towrope, I struggled to shut the cabin door. Many gallons of sea water had rushed into the cabin and, as always in these conditions, the very things that one feels must be secure had come crashing down and were now swilling about in the bilges.

We were really tossed about in the entrance to the harbour and even inside, where it became marginally calmer, the swell continued to knock us against the piles at the outer end, where we were obliged to moor. It was hard to believe that we had left on a perfectly calm morning barely an hour before, and that now there was a good gale blowing.

Laurie and Don joined us within the hour for breakfast, and as they munched they predicted that a blow like this could last as long as five days. They also recommended that we get the help of a serious tug to tow us across the Channel, as a repetition of what had happened that morning would be the end for us. Don, whose face is so weatherbeaten that he is supposed to be able to turn into the north wind and so disturb it by his looks that it turns round and blows in the opposite direction, sat sucking on his delicate pipe and grunting advice about the North Foreland and the tide that races there. They set off into the teeth of the storm to go back to their boatyard in Oare Creek and I watched them go with a great deal of admiration, as their rusty old tug leapt about like a sailing dinghy in the waves, which by now were breaking over the harbour wall and spraying our decks with a mixture of sand, gravel and salt.

Ray and I decided that it would be foolhardy to try to cross the world's busiest shipping lane on our own: the realities of what might happen had been brought home to us that morning, and so I called Ray's old employer, Alan Jubb, to see if he would bring his tug the *Sir Aubrey* down to Whitstable and take us across to Calais. As luck would have it he was towing a small oil platform down to the Medway when I reached him on his mobile telephone. He agreed to come the next day.

Whitstable is still a very pretty little town with its distinctive weatherboarded shacks along the front, and a foreshore which seems to stretch for miles when the tide is out. I talked to Eileen who runs the Sea Salter company, the oldest corporate body in the land. She told me that most of her work now is cleansing molluscs in huge tanks full of purified sea water. I was astonished to see that there were quite a few large clams with shells at least six inches across, which I guessed had come from North America. Apparently they are only found in Southampton Water and it is thought that they must have dropped off the bottom of transatlantic liners or been thrown out of the portholes by chefs clearing out their old shellfish at the end of their journey. The Whitstable native oyster is becoming a very rare beast nowadays. Its decline started in the 1920s when the oyster beds were decimated by disease, and ever since they have been struggling against the pollution from the factories on the Swale. On the other hand the Portuguese oyster seems to thrive, and Eileen sells them for a mere 25p each, compared to the pound she would charge for the native variety, which are juicier and look like an oyster should.

I went round to see the original Wheeler's seafood bar. This was established in the 1870s to sell fresh seafood to the public, and was started by an oyster fisherman, Mr Wheeler, and his wife. Delia, a direct descendant, who looks just like Queen Victoria, but with flaming red hair and a manner to match, sold me a couple of live lobsters and some native oysters, as I thought Ray and I should have some sort of culinary adventure after our dismal maritime experience earlier. She also sold me an oyster knife and showed me how to open the shell, which is really quite hard even when you know how. You have to attack them with the blunt, stubby knife just a little to one side of the hinge. Once the blade is inside, you give a little wriggle which cuts the muscle and allows you to remove the shell. It needs practice.

I had been taught how to execute lobsters in the most humane way in my youth, by a splendid North Californian woman who lived in Cornwall. She showed me how to push the tip of a special broad-bladed fisherman's knife, called a Green River knife, into the shell at the front of the head and cut briskly down the creature's body. They die far more painlessly like this than in boiling water. Grilled, they were delicious, and, as we ate, Ray and I discussed plans for the arrival of the *Sir Aubrey* on the next day. While neither of us actually came out with it, I think we both knew in our hearts that we were going to be stuck in this very uncomfortable berth for some days, pitching and tossing in the swell which the north wind was pushing straight into the harbour, which was now stuffed with other ships sheltering from the storm.

It was early evening before the *Sir Aubrey* forced its way through the now dramatic seas. Alan Jubb and Mac, his toothless and ancient skipper, had come down from the Medway and decided that they would be sheltered if they came along the Swale, but even they were amazed by how lumpy the sea was at the entrance to Whitstable Harbour. We had a short talk and it became clear that with the falling barometer, we would be stuck in the harbour for at least three days. Alan and Mac decided to go home till the weather improved and Ray joined them. I was left by myself to enjoy the pleasures of lying alongside a wall in a serious swell, which I am afraid were precious few.

I found myself struggling with my impatience to get on with the journey, while worrying that even with a large tug towing us we could get caught in a bad squall and sink the *Leo*, unless we waited for settled weather. I listened to almost every forecast and noted the slightest nuance in barometric pressure but it was clear that there would be no improvement before Alan and Ray were due back. The delay gave me a moment to dream about what it would be like over the Channel and into the calm waters of the canals. I began to plan our route. I decided that the journey would provide a perfect opportunity to visit Bruges, which I had heard called the 'Venice of the North'. Many say, too, that Belgian cooking is better than French. I dreamed of moules, *frites* and choc-olate mousse as I tackled beans and bacon at the local sand-blown café. The facilities for cooking on the barge were very good indeed but I didn't feel inclined to try cooking for myself as the boat lurched against the wooden piles of the harbour wall.

The crew returned and we decided that if the forecast was accurate we would leave on the morning tide, at eight o'clock. Ray went over the *Leo*, stopping up all her cocks and screwing down the hatches, as the stern of the tug would be under water or at least awash for most of the trip. He sealed the door from the inside and climbed out of a window. All the wire strops were left ready for the morning.

After a night of little sleep, spent listening to weather forecasts and phoning various weather centres, I decided that we should go, provided that Mac and Alan Jubb agreed once they had sniffed the air – which they did. We made up the tow with the *Sir Aubrey* followed by the barge and then the *Leo*. Alan made up the towrope and attached the rope to the big tug with a very clever Swedish shackle which, as well as the normal U-shaped shackle and pin, had a collar: this made coupling up heavy rope very much simpler. About 150 feet of multiplaited rope, three inches in diameter, was made ready to pay out as soon as we left harbour. The barge was connected to the tug's towrope by a wire halter and the same arrangement was used for the *Leo*.

Ray and I stayed aboard the *Leo* until we were out of the harbour, to make quite sure that all was well and that she was not taking any water. I can't say that I was sorry to see the last of Whitstable Harbour, though I must say I found the town very attractive. The power of the *Sir Aubrey* became apparent as soon as she got under way. The *Leo*, being tail-end-Charlie, swung about like a weight at the end of a pendulum, and we had to rearrange the wire halter on the bows: all the weight was on the metal eyes in the superstructure through which the wire ropes passed, and was actually pulling the steel bulwark away from the deck. Once this was done, Ray and I clambered from one heaving vessel to the next, checked that the Citroën 2CV which we had strapped on the deck of the barge was quite secure, and then made the final leap on to the *Sir Aubrey*, known to the more irreverent river folk on the Thames as the 'Strawberry'. Ray explained to me that when jumping from boat to boat, it was essential to keep your head forward. This, apparently, makes one as sure-footed as a mountain goat. Concentrating on keeping my head forward, I leapt and landed in a heap on the tug's deck.

In the wheelhouse it was remarkably quiet. The tow was strung out satisfactorily behind us and the sea was, for the time being, very nearly flat calm. We pondered over the charts and decided we would make our final decision about whether to go down on the inside of the Goodwin Sands or straight across the Channel, once we got to the infamous North Foreland. The tide is a crucial factor in small-ship navigation but unfortunately it only runs the right way on any voyage for a given period, and so it is vital to make sure that one has planned one's trajectory correctly. We knew that to have the tide with us while we crossed the Channel, we would have to be passing the tide races off the North Foreland when they were in their most confused state. And so it came to pass – with a vengeance.

We were heading for a favourite buoy of mine called the Elbow, from where, if we were to make the crossing straight, we had to turn on a course of 160 degrees towards the south-east. Suddenly, the sea, which had been behaving itself hitherto, started to toss us about as if to see whether our towrope was strong enough. The poor little *Leo* was being

Rotherhithe, London, where it all began.

The *Leo* girds her loins at Greenwich.

Laurie Tester (left) and Don Grover, the wise men of Whitstable.

Chatham Dockyard, once Britain's smartest mooring.

Choppy seas off North Forelands, heading into the Channel.

The American ammunition ship *Montgomery*, too dangerous to demolish.

The competition, Calais.

Layered car cake in Belgium.

flicked about on the end of the line and taking a good deal of water, and the bows of the *Sir Aubrey* were dipping under each wave as she surged forward. Mac, who was at the helm, grinned toothlessly and reduced the engine revolutions until our motion became a little more sedate. Then, as suddenly as our ordeal had started, the sun came out and turned the sea bright blue.

We could see calmer water ahead and behind us the white cliffs of Dover shone bright in the morning sun. It was such a perfect sight, the big ships in the sun, the blue water and the merest hint of the Cap Gris Nez on the horizon. We decided to head straight for Calais – the further off from England, the nearer 'tis to France. Ahead of us lay the East Goodwin Lightship and a little to its right I could see the surf breaking over the treacherous sands. We called the Dover Coastguard to tell them of our intentions. A cultivated woman's voice came on the air, took the details of our strange convoy and told us to proceed.

When we reached the Downs, the spot in the Channel which marks the handover point to the Calais Coastguard, we were called by a man with a delicious French accent. The speaker was extremely surprised that we were such a small convoy, but he controlled his disappointment and gave us permission to proceed to the Calais Harbour entrance, which we estimated we would reach in another three hours, after a seven-hour crossing. By this time we were in the deepest part of the Channel and, surprisingly, the sea had become calm. The only time that we started to pitch and toss was when we were hit by the wash of a large vessel. This always caught us by surprise because the surge arrives long after you think it will, by which time you've forgotten to expect it. We could hear the big ships that we passed remarking on 'that heap of shit'. I wondered why all the radio operators on the British merchant fleet seemed to be from Glasgow. I thought back to those storm-tossed days of waiting in Whitstable Harbour and marvelled at how changeable the sea could be. Here we were on the most perfect spring day in the middle of the Channel, all those months of planning and nights of worrying were over. I felt a huge surge of confidence and almost delirious happiness. I had crossed my Rubicon and decided it was the moment to hoist our French courtesy flag on the *Sir Aubrey's* mast.

By now, we could see the famous clock tower of Calais but were not yet close enough to read the face of the clock through our binoculars. Low on the horizon behind us was the grey shape of a French customs launch travelling at great speed towards us. I suppose they had been alerted to our arrival and had set out from their base in Boulogne. Before long they were close beside us and were giving us the once-over. I think they thought that we were really too unlikely to be running drugs in boats like these, but they were taking no chances and never took their eyes off us, in case we were throwing suspect packets overboard. The last couple of miles before you arrive in Calais are always very choppy, and the euphoria of being out on the high seas soon gave way to a feeling of great relief at being in the safety of Calais Port. As we passed the tide race at the breakwater, the current got hold of the tow and very nearly smashed the *Leo* into the harbour wall, or so it seemed, but Mac managed to aim off enough and disaster was averted by inches.

Once inside the harbour, the radio told us to stop so that a Sealink Ferry could come dashing in. None of us had noticed this huge ship come steaming up behind us. When it had passed we were given a berth in the tidal harbour and as soon as we were tied up our friends from the customs launch came alongside in their inflatable dinghy. They were dressed in woolly hats and jerseys but they were far from cuddly. Their leader carefully pulled his jersey down over his revolver, but not till he had made quite sure that I had seen he was armed. When they saw we were innocent, they looked at all our passports, became very cheery, told us we had to go to the land-based customs and wished us a good trip. They were not a group to cross: I should imagine that there is very little drug-smuggling by sea on that part of the French coast.

CHAPTER TWO

Calais to Bruges

A simple customs clearance was the last thing that I expected, but a worldly-wise young man stamped our papers without delay and wished us a good stay in France. I had decided that we should celebrate after our triumphant crossing, and as all British born before 1950 think that French cooking is the only thing to be taken seriously in France, that and a bit of ooh-la-la, we went to what my comrades thought looked like a suitable place. They chose a newly done-up rip-off joint where we had a dull meal and gallons of beer. My friends enjoyed themselves: in truth we could have eaten much better and probably had a lot more fun at a less glitzy place in the old part of town, but I wasn't in the mood for argument.

After dinner, when I think we were all a little the worse for wear, we moved the boats from the tidal basin into the locked-in port basin of Calais. Here we moored next to a Russian timber ship and watched while curious eyes peered at us from portholes. I was impressed by the number of radio antennae such a workaday craft seemed to need in order to go about its trade in massive logs. I'm not sure that you can be breathalysed for being in charge of a barge, but had anyone come around with a bag to blow in, I don't think any of us would have got away with it. There was a great deal of fumbling with ropes and much tripping, but no harm was done.

The next day the *Sir Aubrey* left to go back to the Thames and we waved her goodbye as we moved into the first of the very many locks we would pass before reaching our destination. The curious thing about the lock in Calais is that you descend from sea level. The great sand dunes thrown up by the sea have made a barrier from Cap Gris Nez to the Belgian coast, which means that the sea at high tide is about two metres above the countryside that stretches eastwards behind the town. Calais has always been a place of refuge for the British. Emma Hamilton ran here from her creditors; the Scarlet Pimpernel, whenever possible, slipped through the fingers of his arch enemy, Chauvelin, here; and it was a few miles up the coast at Dunkerque that the British Expeditionary Force was forced off the beaches in the Second World War.

So many British have passed through Calais, it's a miracle that it has retained any Frenchness at all, though once one gets away from the hypermarkets and into the smaller streets there are some very pleasant areas. We moored in a little basin not far from the famous clock tower and filled our water tanks from a stopcock we found in the grass. Luckily the pressure was very good: we needed to wash all the salt off the metal work as soon as possible, as it can be very corrosive. Counting the damage from the trip across the Channel, the only thing that had gone badly wrong was that, although we had screwed drain covers into the recessed ports down the side of the barge, we had not adequately tightened the porthole over the sink. I had thought that it wouldn't really matter, as it would just drip into the steel bowl. I was wrong. With the pounding the barge had taken coming across the Channel, enough water had been forced through this tiny crack to leave a pool an inch deep over the entire floor of the barge. By now we had managed to dry most of it up, but there was still a good deal under the floorboards and I knew it would start to rot the wood if we didn't get the boat completely dry; also, if the damp were not tackled, we might start getting electrical trouble – probably the greatest problem that a mariner can face on the canals, or so I naively thought at the time. The solution, I decided, was to get a blower heater.

The generator started easily and the blower heater was switched on. Taking the 2CV off the barge, we went for a drive around the town and did some serious shopping. One thing we needed was some of Michel Sandrin's excellent maps of the waterways of France and Belgium. They are very cleverly laid out so that they really make sense from the water, which makes it easier to estimate – barring incident – where one might get to each night. The other thing that we required was some heavy-duty cable to run an electrical supply to the radio. This consumed a lot more power than I had anticipated. It worked well whilst it was receiving signals, but as soon as I started to transmit, it activated the electronic device that gauged if there was not enough current, and the set was switched off. I wanted to fix this before we went too much further because I knew that it was essential to be able to speak to the lock-keepers at some of the bigger locks, so they knew when to expect you.

In the late afternoon we set off from Calais with just enough time to get through the first lock before it closed for the night at 7.30 p.m. Leaving Calais we passed through two automatic bridges. This was easy for us, but there was a small, plastic French boat which was having a lot of trouble, because it wasn't big enough to set off the signalling device. This required a big metal object like a barge to pass through its beam, so the skipper was very grateful to be able to follow us through. The usual bonhomie ensued, but our encounter was short-lived as he was able to go much faster than us. We soon lost sight of him as he sped down the long straight stretches of the Canal de Calais – built by Louis XIV and probably one of the oldest canals in Europe.

The first true canal lock was opened by an unusually pretty girl. Ray inquired whether this standard of pulchritude was normal, but I'm afraid I had to assure him that it was not. That night we tied up in a little town called Watten on the main canal from the coalfields of Northern France to Dunkerque. We now had the choice of whether to go north, following the canal through Dunkerque and then along the coast to Bruges, or to go via the River Lys and St Omer to the south. I decided that the industrialization of the Dunkerque route would be a lot less pleasant than the Lys. I wanted, in any case, to have a look at the Anderton lift at Les Fontinettes.

The next morning was one of those that make any trip magic. There was mist on the canal and sun on the trees lining the bank. The local *boulangerie* supplied us with fresh croissants and away we went. The good old *Leo* was chugging along very happily and we didn't appear to have any electrical problems. Then, quite suddenly, the moment was gone. On the bank, on a crash barrier by the road which ran along the side of the canal, sat a teenage boy in obvious distress. On the road lay all the sad, telltale signs of a recent accident: oil, shards of glass. Later, when I inquired what had happened, I found that two young coach drivers, driving very close together and much too fast, resulting in one coach crashing into the back of the other, had killed seventeen people including the boy's best friend. I felt I had intruded on his grief, but we were soon gone round the bend, probably never to pass that way again. I hope he never forgets his friend.

Les Fontinettes is a massive lock with a thirteen-metre lift, which can take barges of up to 1300 tons. Before this giant was constructed, a Scots engineer called James Anderton had, in 1887, built a lift which did the same thing for the standard French barge. The barges are sealed into one of two water-filled basins which rise and fall under high-pressure hydraulic control. At first sight, one's instinct is to assume that the basin with the barge in it must be heavier than the one with just water, but in fact a boat displaces its own weight in the water, so they balance perfectly. The mayor of the district is doing his best to preserve this masterpiece of riveted steel, but no one is very interested and I'm afraid it will not be long before it is condemned as unsafe.

45

Ray and I took the car off and went for a trip to St Omer – a pretty little town, passed by the hordes on the motor routes without so much as a glance. The canal which used to pass through the middle of the town has been closed for a decade or two, but it is still a bit of France as it must have been before the 1939–45 war. I watched an old man buy his baguette and balance it on the handlebars of his bike whilst he did up his cycle clips, which he had taken off his trousers before going into the *boulangerie*. I wondered why it had been so important to him. Perhaps it was just habit or perhaps the woman who ran the shop had a certain twinkle in her eye. Buying bread in France is a very serious business and an anchor to the real world. In many places, the average family will buy bread twice a day, unless they shop at the local supermarket where the loaves come in a clingfilm sheath and taste of rubber.

We set off again down the wide Grand Gabarit canal, and soon realized why it had been built so wide. Coming towards us was the most enormous tow: four really massive barges pushed by a huge power unit. We crept to the side of the canal but even so there was hardly enough room for us both to pass. The strong undertow seemed to draw us on to the barges but at the last minute pushed us away again. As we passed the wheelhouse the skipper gave us a cheery wave. Palely, I fluttered my hand in return. It is much wiser to listen for the arrival of these monsters on the radio, which gives you time to find a wide place to lurk whilst they go by.

The River Lys looks a lot more enticing on the map than it is on the ground. For the first few miles it was very pretty, with quaint, old, manually operated lift-bridges and cross *éclusiers*, but soon we approached Merville, which is no more than an average industrial town in Northern France. Factories lined the banks and debris of all sorts floated on the river. We found a field outside the town, just as the sun was going down, and decided to stop. I went ashore with the

46

sledgehammer, drove in a couple of stakes and hitched our mooring warps over them. One of the cardinal rules about mooring anywhere on rivers or canals is always to have two lines out. I have been cursed many times for only making fast the bows, which means that when a barge goes past the undertow pulls the stern of your boat out and it bounces against the other vessel. The other golden rule is to start looking for somewhere to tie up early in the day: if you don't, you invariably end up in a really beastly place, next to a chemical plant.

We crossed the Belgian border soon after we got under way the next day. Our papers were inspected by a morose-looking gentleman who was leaving this posting, where he had been for the last twelve years, the very next day. As he was going through my papers a band of his colleagues came bounding into this sleepy little customs post. They merrily produced some bottles of Calvados and we all drank to the gloomy *douanier* who explained that the equally morose fish in the plastic bowl on the window ledge was the last surviving fish this year in the grossly polluted Lys.

Whether it was the Calvados or just plain stupidity, I made a wrong turning on the canal and had entered a lock before I realized my mistake. Coming out backwards caused a certain amount of ribald comment from the local barge community who were understandably annoyed at having to wait while this daft English boat sorted itself out. In the confusion I chatted to Freddie, a Belgian *batelier*, who was manoeuvring his barge, the *Helga*, with very considerable skill. He told me that his family had been in the *marinier* trade since the seventeenth century. He was the fifth generation and lived with his pretty wife Helga (his barge was romantically called after her) and their two children aboard their floating home. The children were having a holiday the next day so they were to be picked up in a taxi from school and brought to the barge that evening. The *Helga* was carrying 300 tons of soya pellets for cattlefeed to a distribution point near Lille. Freddie and

Helga were to arrive at their dock that evening, and were looking forward to a few days' rest before they got another cargo. They clearly had good contacts, but told me that they sometimes had to wait for up to three weeks for a cargo from a freight bureau.

I thought Armentières was worth a visit, so we stopped for a few hours. It was hard to realize that the area we were passing through so peacefully had been the battleground in almost every European war for the last two millennia. The city, flattened in the First World War, was bustling, bright, and swinging with young and extremely kissable *mademoiselles* (the original mademoiselle from Armentières won notoriety, as the song has it, by stealing a barber's pole and chopping it up for firewood). The Belgians have obviously found the secret of Common Market prosperity by providing the Market headquarters and, no doubt, collecting a sizable rent. They also manage to have more television channels than anyone else in Europe – including all the British channels for which, apparently, they pay nothing at all.

Under way again, we soon came to a halt in a long queue of barges in Dienze. A railway bridge about thirty miles ahead had been raised and the canal was to be blocked for three days. At least that is what I was told by the barge people we were moored behind. I knew from experience that non-professionals like ourselves never get told the truth in case they get in the queue ahead of the regular barges. I could see that we were in for a long wait, so Ray decided to go back to London for a couple of days, and as we were only six hours from Bruges, we arranged to meet there.

I went to the station to help Ray with translation and buy some stores, and when I got back to the boat, hardly two hours later, the queue of twenty barges had disappeared as if by magic.

I set off by myself the next day – something that I had promised myself not to do, but the canal to Bruges was very

wide and there was only one lock. I was also able to use the
VHF radio telephone to make link calls to London. This
involved having a radio operator's licence, a maritime VHF
radio, and a licence for the radio. After that, providing your
ship is within the range of the resident transmitter, in this
case Radio Antwerp, it is relatively easy to make a call. One
of the pleasant things about the system is that it takes at least
six months for the bills to come through. It took quite a long
time for me to be able to roll the necessary alphabet round
my tongue, however. Lima Echo Oscar November Tango
Yankee November Echo was how I had to spell my ship's
name; Mike Alpha Delta Mike Fiver our callsign. For some
reason it is usual amongst the waveband fraternity to add
little flourishes to the end of certain words, like the 'r' on the
end of five.

My journey to Bruges was uneventful and took me along
wide canals, the high banks on either side blocking the view
of Flanders field. When the banks disappeared Bruges came
into view. A once very prosperous city whose fortunes were
based on the wool trade, it was preserved from developments
in the nineteenth and twentieth centuries by its parlous state.
Now, because it is so astonishingly unspoiled, it is in real
danger of being stared to death by the millions of tourists
who flock there every year. The lace that Bruges is famous
for is made in Taiwan and sold to visitors desperate for some
kind of souvenir that they can buy in the five minutes they
have been allowed by their tour operators for shopping.
Mercifully, the vast coaches that bring these bewildered
sheep are not able to get into the middle of the town because,
as Art Buchwald wrote to his mother, the streets of Bruges,
like those of Venice, are full of water.

I found a berth alongside a mown and grassy bank under
one of the three windmills in Bruges. Charlotte and Bernard,
boat dreamers from London, were there to catch my ropes
and help me make fast. They had built a boat in Holland the
year before, had just made their first trip over the Channel,

and were now on their way to the Mediterranean for the rest of their days. This was their plan, a dream which would almost certainly not be realized because they both had far too much energy to sit around in the sun for long periods. However it is dreams of this sort that keep boat-builders building boats which are becoming increasingly like suburban houses. Their floating palazzo was called the *Kyamanzi*, a name from Zululand meaning a home on the water.

I found my way into Bruges through the neat little park which had so thoughtfully been provided as a mooring. As I strolled through the trees, I discovered about sixty men sitting silently on stools beside wicker baskets. It took me some time to realize that they were a group of pigeon-racing enthusiasts, awaiting the start of a race which they clearly took very seriously. I longed to ask them about their hobby, but speech would have been as much disapproved of as in the library of the Travellers' Club. Carrier pigeons were used to bring the news of the result of the Battle of Waterloo to the House of Rothschild in Paris, so I suppose the pigeons have been navigating their way through Belgium for centuries. How they find their way will always be a mystery to me.

I wandered through the pretty streets, which were full of the most surprising things. In one shop, which didn't look like a shop at all, I found Willi, who had been a mechanic on a large farm. He agreed to try to mend the *Leo*'s hydraulic pump that lifted the crane arm, and also all the temperature gauges. Talking to him wasn't the easiest thing because he spoke French with the guttural accent of the Flemish. I did discover that he was a pigeon fancier, however, and he mournfully told me of a misfortune that his pigeon-racing compatriots had suffered. Apparently thousands of racing pigeons had set off on some race the previous year and had not been seen since. No one has any idea what happened to them, though it's thought that perhaps they flew into some freak magnetic field and became disorientated. He finished my job remarkably quickly and left everything working.

While he was still at it, I took the dinghy and rowed round the canals of Bruges. When I started it was calm and peaceful but suddenly the tourist launches started to run: that made my progress uncomfortable because the drivers didn't expect to find anyone rowing round these narrow canals and there was much cursing as they had to slow down to let me pass. The drivers were all the same type, handsome and sporting heavy dark glasses, spouting hackneyed commentary about the buildings they passed, and always ready to give that little extra attention to the lonely female tourist. By midday the town was full. The great landcruisers had brought their load of tourists for the day and they swayed through the alleys being harangued by their group leader. So much information, so many languages, so many heads swivelling to pointed fingers. There does come a point when there are simply too many people in one place at one time.

I tied up the dinghy, and went into the Church of Our Lady to have a look at the splendid Michelangelo they have there. It had been bought by a member of a Bruges merchant family while he was working in Italy, brought home and presented to the church. In fact it is one of the very few Michelangelos that have found their way out of Italy. I found it extremely beautiful and happily paid my entrance fee to have a closer look. What a nice little earner it must be for the church, rather like having *The Sound of Music* in the library of a film distributor.

I found myself walking through the car park to avoid the crowds, when I noticed a mechanical-organ museum. The door was opened by a fresh-faced woman whose gaiety was quite infectious. She took me to her boss, explaining that she was not yet qualified to do the tour. As I was the only person in the museum the tour didn't seem to be very important but there was no way I could see that I was going to be allowed to

51

wander round this enormous collection of fairground organs alone. As I waited for Mrs Hilbergen to descend from her office, which overlooked the collection, the girl who had let me in started up the largest of the organs with the triumphal march from *Aida*. In that confined space the decibels were all-embracing and it was impossible not to smile: this place is to be strongly recommended when feeling glum. Mrs Hilbergen, a briskly agreeable woman, had been an accountant in Ostend until the company that employed her acquired this collection of mechanical instruments from an enthusiast. She had been put in charge of the place and was turning what could have been a fairly staid exhibition into a place of entertainment. As *Aida* came to an end she started up her most famous organ, the Black Cat, with the 'Violletten Waltz,' and taking me by the hand, suggested that we waltzed on the two-metre-square piece of dance floor. This was not at all what I had expected, and it proved to be very agreeable.

The infectious gaiety of the music and my two companions made the morning rush by, and I was very sorry to leave when a coach party of old-age pensioners arrived from Brussels. As I left, my friends were giving the pensioners a blast of 'J'attendrai' on the big organ, which had the old boys and girls in each other's arms on the minuscule patch of floor in no time.

They make delicious chocolates in Bruges, mostly by hand. The process is not at all simple. The biggest drawback to making them at home is getting the chocolate to shine. This only happens if the temperature of the chocolate is very, very precisely controlled. A tenth of a degree centigrade can make all the difference between a glistening triumph or what looks like a dusty old choc from last year's Christmas boxes. The other closely guarded secret these *chocolatiers* pass through the generations to each other is the exact blend of cocoa beans. The buying of these beans takes place at the London Cocoa Market and the right blend of bean at the right price is all important. Once the beans are bought they are sent to an outside factory to be turned into chocolate, as the plant required is far too expensive for the small trader. The chocolate is then melted down to exactly the right temperature and poured into moulds. Once the thin layer of the walls of the chocolate has set in the moulds, the centres are filled with all sorts of delicious things and then another layer of chocolate is poured on the top. Though this may sound frivolous, in Bruges it is a *métier* that is taken very seriously indeed. But alas, chocolates and chips go straight to the hips.

The other major pastime in Belgium is drinking beer, of which there are untold varieties – some stronger than Scotch whisky, or so it seemed. After a glass, I found myself talking to the most beautiful girl in the land as she leant across the counter at the Café Vlissinghe, where she was helping her mother who had been running the place for the last forty years. She was well over six feet tall and built extremely neatly. Her husband, who was an engineer on a supertanker, was due back the next day after six months at sea and she was positively purring with expectation. '*Leontyne*, what a beautiful name,' she sighed, when I told her the name of my boat. I fell for her, her pub and for Belgium at that moment, which was probably what the mischievous monks who brewed the dark and dangerous beer I was quaffing had in mind.

The elegant carillon towering over Bruges has forty-seven bells and is the biggest in the world, according to the carilloner, Aimé Lambaert. Aimé also confided that his friends called him 'Lovely' – odd, as he looked like Abraham Lincoln and was a muscular man from playing his carillon and climbing the 365 steps up to the loft two or three times a day. He sits at his machine, which looks like a loom, and hits the keys with the sides of his hands. He told me that he heard the music through the vibrations in his arms, because his loft is below the belfry. When he plays, the keys that he hits pull down wires attached to the clappers inside the bells. He obviously felt extremely powerful up there in his loft, spreading his magnificent peals over sleepy Bruges. In the belfry itself there is a huge bronze drum made in the seventeenth century, with small pegs in its perforated surface like an enormous musical box. Aimé Lambaert changes these pegs every two years so that the bells play a different tune on the hour. When the drum plays, the bells are struck by hammers on the outside, which makes a subtly different sound to that made by the clappers.

It all sounded powerfully perfect to me as I watched Bruges' big parade on Ascension Day. The parade itself was a pleasantly homely affair which had attracted thousands of tourists from all over the world. Religious in content, it revolved round the usual tales and the parading of an authentic relic. This was carried in turn by a group of elderly high priests, who were only able to carry the heavily ornate gold casket for a few steps before passing it on to one of their colleagues. Somehow the parade organizers were able to cope with this stopping and starting and kept the parade moving forward. As the relic came through the main square under the carillon, Aimé Lambaert had his bi-annual treat and pealed the victory bell (what Belgian victory was commemorated by this bell was not explained).

The *Leo* was now beginning to work as she should: the oil and water gauges had been fixed by Willi, and I had bought a new outboard engine with a little more power for the dinghy. Ray was still in London when I set off on a sparkling spring day for the south. As I glided past the fortress towers of old Bruges, I watched a family of tiny moorhens being shepherded by their mother as they bobbed about in the *Leo*'s wash. The time I had spent in Bruges had been full of interest, but the joy of being on board the *Leo* again and under way on such a day had me singing tunelessly, songs of my youth. The excitement of adventure and not being certain where or how the day would end still caught me by surprise.

CHAPTER THREE

Bruges to Agimont

Soon after midday, an incident occurred that raised the adrenalin to almost unacceptable limits. A pusher barge with a large tow was coming towards me and from behind a Dutch barge was hurrying down the canal. The Dutchman decided to overtake just as the other barge was passing. There wasn't really enough room but in spite of a lot of horn blowing on my part, the Dutchman pushed past; as he did so the turbulence sucked the *Leo* on to him and even though I slowed down, I was stuck to him and drawn alongside in some horrible marine embrace until we had passed the other barge. We parted, shaking fists at each other. Just like motorists, I thought. The trouble with dreams of vengeance on canals is that you inevitably meet the offending barge at the next lock, when you have to be ready with the customary cheery wave: I couldn't pointedly shut the wheelhouse door to show ill humour, since I had to steer from the deck.

That night I stopped at Kortrijk, where Ray rejoined me. We moored next to a barge with swaying palm trees painted on the hull, which announced itself as the *Waikiki Disco*. I had a quick look to see whether I would be awake all night with the rhythm of the South Seas but clearly the proprietors had either fallen on hard times or it was too early in the season for grass skirts. Next to the bridge ahead of us was a mobile *frites* shop. It was clearly very well thought of as streams of expensive motorcars drove up for their portions of *frites* cooked in rendered horse fat. Wandering round this prosperous town and gazing into several shop windows, which were devoted to silver golf balls turned into lighters and other icons of our consumer society, I found myself quite suddenly in the quiet courtyard of a *Béguinage*. The Beguines were an order founded in England in the middle ages, for girls of families who could not afford to pay the dowries that the nunneries required to shelter their daughters. The girls who went to a *Béguinage* were subjected to a regime very similar to a nun's except that every day they went out to work, always in pairs, in the local community.

As I walked round these calm and beautiful courtyards, I realized I was being watched furtively by a pair of black beady eyes concealed in the shadowy doorway of the chapel. I approached, but as I did so I heard the faintest scuffle, and their owner had disappeared by the time I reached the door. Intrigued now, I went to have a look in all the doorways, until I found one that had the sounds of an harmonium coming from it. I knocked and a tiny Beguine opened the door. She told me that she and the pair of eyes I had seen were the last two Beguines in Kortrijk, in this establishment which had been here for at least four hundred years. She was very frail and so asked me into her tiny cell so she could sit down while she told me of her work and her life. She was practically blind now but she had such a sweet smile that it was a pleasure to listen to her telling her life story.

She had come to the *Béguinage* when she was eighteen in 1939, and giggled as she told me of the first veil she had to wear as a novice, which was so restricting that she was only able to look forwards. No glancing out of the corner of her eye. She told me proudly that her grandfather had been in the special French Unit of the Papal Guard, of how she had learned to play the guitar and harmonium to entertain the sick and how happily she had given her life to the service of God and his creatures. The *Béguinage* was now occupied by elderly ladies who had come to spend the rest of their days in a sheltered environment, and she left me to go and see that they were comfortable. This tiny, cheerful person had a profound effect on me and as I left and walked back to the

Leo past the shops with the gold dinner services, I wondered at the state of our society today and how long it would be before some greedy property developer would put forward a proposal to turn the *Béguinage* into a block of offices with a hostel for old people beside it.

Puzzled by Kortrijk I left through the centre of the town along a beautifully built brick wall by the canalside. The bricks in Belgium seem to be smaller than the good old London stock brick. I hope this splendid piece of canal construction does not get swept away by the enlargements that the Belgian government is making to the waterways system. In the heat of the day, we came to a lock alongside which an enormous new lock was being built, big enough for ships of 1300 tons, and which would do away with four of the existing locks. Either the Belgians have found a cupboard full of Common Market money, or they must very sensibly believe that there is a future for cheap transport by water. The system these new locks use is worth recounting: the locks themselves are so vast that, when they are emptied, an enormous cubic metreage of water is lost, which causes serious problems for the reaches further up the canal or river. The modern systems have enormous electrical pumps which compensate for this by pumping the water out of the lock and into tanks nearby, or into the upper reach. When the lock is filled again the water is pumped back into the lock.

The portly lock-keeper who showed me round this marvel told me of a Czech friend of his who had recently taken his car to the USSR. Normally a sober person, this friend had returned with over ninety tickets for motoring offences. Apparently the Soviets had decided that he was a person worth keeping an eye on and had placed a bug on his car. The friend could not imagine why, in the middle of nowhere, a traffic policeman would invariably spring out at him and hand him a speeding ticket. Apparently he did not have to pay the fines, but it made him extremely cautious.

That night we had a setback. We arrived at Bossuit, an

unmemorable place, and the lock-keeper asked me whether I should like to stop on the upper side of the lock or the lower. When I said that I was going to continue he told me that the lock at Espierres had been closed as a barge had run into one of the lock gates, and that there was nothing to do but wait whilst a new gate was installed, which would take at least two days. I unloaded the 2CV and went to have a look at the damage, which was quite impressive. A huge mobile crane had lifted the mangled gate out and laid it on the ground; a new gate was to be installed the following day. The force of a 1300-ton barge, even when it is creeping into the lock at a snail's pace, can be quite enormous. If a checking rope slips or snaps, or a gear cable parts, there is nothing that can be done to stop it crashing into the gates. Nothing, that is, unless you are German: the Germans have a very efficient system for lowering a huge wire hawser across the lock, about two metres from the gates opposite the entry side. It is raised before the gates are opened, of course, but it's strong enough to stop these very expensive accidents from happening.

All round the lock were waiting barges. Some of the wealthier *bateliers* had taken their cars off with the extensive lift arms that they had installed, and driven off. Others were painting and scraping their main asset. No wonder their barges look so spick-and-span: the number of man hours that go into lacquering the decks with special varnish, clearing every speck of rust off the hull, and keeping the paint fresh, must be enormous. Delays of this kind are very annoying however, because the *bateliers* can be penalized for not delivering their cargoes on the appointed day.

The canal was opened sooner than expected and we made our way through Tournai, which lies at the southernmost part of Flanders. The river, with all its heavy barge traffic, runs right through the middle of the town and makes a fine sight. I went into an antique shop on the quay, to have a look at a particularly fine bit of lace in the window, but was sidetracked by some postcards of the town during the 1939–45 war. The streets in which I had been walking had been virtually destroyed by successive American, British and German bombardments. I have often wondered what it must have been like to live in a town that had been invaded and occupied by enemy forces. This is something that neither the British nor the Americans had to experience in either of the World Wars. What would one's attitude have been to the occupying force?

By now we were heading east through the 'cockpit of Europe'. Neat signs from the war graves commissions reminded one of the huge costs of war. From time to time, we could see the rows upon rows of white crosses on the green, rolling countryside. It was hard to imagine that this place was once a sea of mud, where screaming shells replaced the spring birds.

We were now in old canal country and the *Leo* felt at home. The barge traffic was light and when barges passed us they were mere 300-tonners making a short cut to one of the main canals. It soon became apparent why the larger craft did not use this canal, when we were faced with a flight of four Anderton lifts. These marvels of Victorian engineering closed at 5.00 p.m., which is early on the canals, and we were caught at the bottom level. This delay gave us the opportunity to investigate what was causing the vibration we could feel in the propeller shaft. I was quite sure that we had picked up a bit of rope that had entwined round the propeller. Ray and I tried a *very* unsuccessful experiment, namely trying to lift the stern of the *Leo* out of the water with the crane that was installed on the barge. Of course, it was not nearly powerful enough but at least we had made the attempt, because we knew that one of us would have to plunge into the still chilly, murky waters of the canal to feel what was wrong. Ray bravely volunteered and, after some minutes of diving under the *Leo*'s stern, told me that the propeller blades were badly dented by a stone and that we would have to change the propeller as soon as we could. This meant we would have to lift the *Leo* out of the water as it was extremely difficult to change the propeller under water, even with a diver.

In the early morning, we let a barge pass us in the queue, as indeed one should: they have to earn a living and, more to the point, they pay for the use of the canals. Our ascent through Anderton's four masterpieces was uneventful. The lifts are so massively built and kept in such good repair by the authorities that it is surprising that they are not a much bigger tourist attraction, although once the new lift that is under construction at this point on the canal is finished, this will doubtless happen. The new lift will replace the four Anderton lifts and will be capable of taking 1300-ton barges. It stands like some vast blockhouse awaiting another German invasion, this time the invasion of the inevitable superbarges.

We were now up on a plateau and since we had been through a series of lifts, I thought we should visit Belgium's other hydraulic curiosity: the nearby lift at Ronquières which joins the canal from Brussels to the Meuse. This is really a huge bathtub on wheels into which the barges are driven and sealed. The whole apparatus is then allowed to slowly slide down the hill to the canal at the bottom. The bath is checked by a system of massive counterweights and safety devices, but I was nevertheless relieved when the *Leo* was back to the safety of more conventional means of lifting river traffic.

Leaving Ronquières, we came upon a breakdown truck by the side of the canal and a boy with a flag waving at all the passing barges to slow them down. I decided to tie up and see what was going on. As I reached the boy a frogman appeared from the canal and flopped his way up the bank. Mr Van Damme had found himself a job for life clearing the canals of Belgium of 'hot' cars. His method was simple. He would drive down one side of the canal and his assistant would drive down the other, with a steel hawser running between the two vehicles. From time to time, the cable would snag on a car and Mr Van Damme would slip into his wet suit. His first priority was to collect the number plates from the car (I think he was probably paid by the plates). Then he would plunge again, attach a cable around the chassis of the car and winch it up on to the canal bank. I watched him pull a very new looking BMW up on to the bank. He told me that it had probably been in the canal for about six months. I was surprised when he attached the winch cable to the boot of the car to prise it open. 'What do you think is inside?' I asked, thinking of swag, but he explained that the only things of interest that he ever found were live eels. Sadly when the lid of the boot sprung open, it was empty. However, within the hour he had a top-of-the-range Toyota up on the bank and this time the boot disgorged six eels for Mrs Van Damme to cope with. Because of its isolation, this part of the canal was a favourite dumping ground for car thieves, explained my diving friend, who was very proud of his job – though I must say it is not one that I should fancy, especially during the winter.

Charleroi is, from the canal at least, an industrial night-mare. All one could see were huge buildings, chimneys belching clouds of noxious vapour, and bright points of light from molten metal being poured. Welders were repairing a conveyor belt high above and evil clankings and bangings deafened me. The fact that humans are persuaded to work in places like these, inhaling the grime in the air day after day, convinced me of how lucky I was to be merely passing through. Later, in a lock outside Charleroi, I asked the skipper of a tug that was towing a huge barge of liquid mud if there was anything of interest between where we were and Namur. 'It is all very much the same,' was his morose reply.

We wound our way down the Sambre to the Meuse at Namur. Ray was making a little headway with his French and came back triumphantly with some eggs which he had purchased with the aid of the Paul Daniels 'Learn a language by word association' book which he had been studying while

The carillon in Bruges, Venice of the North.

An elegant mooring, Bruges.

Belgium's Côte d'Azur, Dinant.

A 388-wheeler at Ronquières.

at the helm. He had bought the eggs to make one of his famous lighterman's omelettes: none of the salmonella-inhabited, runny, French-style versions for Ray. His were solidly delicious and a real meal in themselves. Already the allure of meals in restaurants had begun to pall. The cost was one factor, but by far the most irksome element in restaurant eating was the time it took to order something and then to eat it. I suppose it is all part of good living, spending ages over a meal and savouring every aspect of its presentation, but the eternal inquiry as to what each dish contained and above all whether it contained any garlic, which made Ray ill, became increasingly tiresome.

We were moored under the magnificent citadel in Namur, which no doubt had had a glorious past, but in the recent World Wars had had only a very short history of combat. It stands perched high on a hill at the junction of the Meuse and the Sambre, and must have looked very daunting to any invaders approaching from the river, but it was attacked from the rear in the First and Second World Wars. The defenders thought they had everything catered for, but were surprised by a parachute attack directly into the middle of the fortified area. Between the *Leo* and the citadel was one of the casinos that earn this part of the country the title 'Belgium's Côte d'Azur'. Ray and I went to see whether we could get into this vast modern gambling hall, but we were not properly dressed and the men on the door obviously did not like the cut of our jib, so we decided to let them keep their money and moved on to Dinant further up the Meuse.

Probably the most knowledgeable man about the nuts and bolts of film making that I know had heard we were in the area and came on board for lunch. Lee Katz has spent most of his life in Hollywood, sometimes writing scripts for Warner Brothers 'B' pictures and sometimes acting as assistant director or producer on major movies. Some were good, some bad and some indifferent but Lee was a true professional who had known all the greats of Hollywood in the golden studio

63

years. He is always amusing company and was in Europe on business of one kind or another. He told me of his days as assistant director on *Casablanca* and of how neither Humphrey Bogart nor Ingrid Bergman had been the first choice for their parts, nor had they wanted to play them, but they, like Claude Rains, were under contract to Jack Warner and had been obliged to make the film. *Casablanca* was entirely shot in the studio, though it has been praised many times for having the authentic feel of the Paris streets just before the war. He told me with some pride that it had been his idea, when the script arrived at the last minute for the final scene in which Bergman and her film husband leave from the airport, to make the studio set look authentic by hiring a group of dwarves to load the plane, and so give the correct perspective. Nobody at the studios ever thought the film would be successful and so even the choice of music was limited to what was cheap and already belonged to Warners. 'As Time Goes By,' Casablanca, Bogart, Bergman and Rains somehow made a magic that will last forever. The film is a brilliant example of how nobody, but nobody, knows what the public will like and respond to before the work has been completed. Lee caught the train to Paris and I was sorry to see his dapper figure disappear with his memories.

As we pushed on up the Meuse we came to the Ardennes. Steep wooded hills swept down to the river's edge, making the landscape look as though someone tidier than I had folded it away in a drawer, like socks. I remembered how my mother who had been a fine watercolourist had explained the principles of the vanishing point to me whilst she was sketching the blue hills of the Nilgiri range in South India. With a few deft brush strokes, she had made the ranges of hills fall behind each other, somehow managing to create a distance on a flat surface. Perspective to me is a truly mysterious subject, but the Meuse in the sunset that evening seemed to wander enticingly up the sky, like the backdrop of a clever ballet set at Covent Garden. At an isolated lock, the lock-keeper told me how worried he was for the magnificent apple tree outside his little house. The tree was covered with blossom but he felt that the weather was sure to be unkind and there would be snow in July which would deny him the obvious bounty that was coming his way. He sold us some free-range eggs and some home-made cider and we felt enormously relieved to be in the deep country away from the roar of industrial Charleroi and the swank of the casino in Namur. The Ardennes on an evening such as this is as beautiful as anywhere that I have travelled. I wonder if the crew of the American tank that has been left beside the road at Agimont appreciated the beauty of the place.

Agimont is a very small hamlet on the border between Belgium and France. There is an agreeable chandler there who caters for the barge people as well as pleasure craft. We refuelled and bought a few items from his shop which was one of those places that has everything stacked away with no apparent order. We started to talk about the tank and the war over an excellent glass of Prunes de Bourgogne (this was the only place I have been able to find it). I wanted to know what it had been like to be a civilian in the war and to have occupying forces in a village of this size. He told me that I should talk to the local schoolmaster who had been at the school in Agimont for forty-four years and remembered both world wars.

The next morning the chandler came to the boat and we walked to the schoolmaster's house. The house was at one end of a neat little terrace of brick houses and had a courtyard at the back. At the side of the court there was the entrance to a living room that was jammed with furniture and an enormous stove which was burning merrily away. The schoolmaster was bright-eyed and very clear-thinking and immediately started to talk about his recollections of seventy-four years before. The old boy had so much authority that the chandler (an ex-pupil) and I sat on the floor spellbound.

He told of how the French army had arrived dressed in the

red and blue uniforms of the Napoleonic pattern with their fixed bayonets glinting in the sun. He told us of how he had helped the soldiers, who had had no field kitchen, to fill their waterbottles and start cooking on fires beside the road. How quickly it all changed, he said. The French were pushed back and the German army of occupation took over.

He described how terrible it had been for civilians in the first war in those parts. There had been many brutalities and reprisals on a much worse scale than in the second war. This was the reason that, as soon as it became clear that the Germans would again overrun the Ardennes in the Second World War, the population immediately left for France. The old man told us how in mid-May, forty-eight years before, the French army had again come along the road through his village and, convinced that there would be no war, had pushed sprigs of lilac down the muzzles of their field artillery. He had gone with the refugees and had returned after a couple of months, to start up the school again, but was infuriated to find that his house had been looted and his prized camera had been taken as well as his mattress – two things which were almost impossible, in those days, to replace.

He spoke with great passion about the inadequacies of the military mind, how little the generals had profited by history, and about the inaccuracies of the bombing and shelling by both sides. The Germans had a large ammunition dump in the forest near Agimont and this had been communicated to the Allies, who bombed the area a number of times but never anywhere near the dump: some of the bombs fell near his school and smashed the windows.

I left the old man's house thinking that I would never be able to understand what it was like to be living in a country that was under occupation. Would one be heroic or passively resistant or, perhaps, collaborate? How did he explain the situation to his pupils then, and how did he place it in historical terms now? In eighty-eight years he had hardly

strayed from this place of, at the most, two thousand inhabitants, and yet he had probably had more real things happen
to him in his life than most people would dream possible.

CHAPTER FOUR

Agimont to Rheims

We left Agimont in a swirling mist and crossed the border back into France without incident. I had decided to donate our coil of manila rope, bought at Chatham Dockyard, to the courageous old schoolteacher, who ran a cultural circle, and had left the huge bundle and a note with the chandler. I hope it was possible to sell it to a passing barge and that the circle could do something with the money.

Our entry to France was at a charming village called Givet. It looked perfectly French with wide avenues, plane trees and men playing *pétanque*. It was hot enough for the umbrellas to be out on the café tables and the drowsiness of summer in France was just beginning. Jauntily I stepped into the customs post and started speaking to the young officer behind the glass partition who took not the slightest notice of me. He never so much as glanced in my direction until a slightly older and less pimply *douanier* arrived. The less pimply one stroked his bumfluff beard as he examined my passport and the ship's papers. The more I explained that we had already entered France once, the more inquisitive they became. It was a Saturday morning and I did not want to be stuck here for the long weekend – it was Pentecost and the locks would be shut for forty-eight hours. I started to become less than my usual patient self but it was like grinding mud. More senior *douaniers* were called and it was decided a thorough search of the boat was to be made after lunch, which was at least something, even though it meant waiting another two hours. Ray, quickly assessing the situation in practical terms, suggested that they were causing the delay on purpose so that they could claim Saturday afternoon overtime.

Ray was clearly cross that the boat should be searched and glowered as the group came on board. The youngest member, who had ignored me when I had arrived at his bureau, had changed into rummage gear for groping around in the bilges. The customs men were obviously hoping that they had stumbled on a major drug-trafficking ring, but became rather unsure of themselves when they got below. Just as they started to take everything apart, their walkie-talkie squawked and they stopped at once, explaining that their big chief was arriving. Fearing the worst, I went up on deck and waited. The chief was a charming man in civilian clothes who told me that he had been pottering around in his garden when the message had come through from these rather over-zealous colleagues that they might have caught a big fish. With enormous Gallic charm he called off the troops and apologized for any delays they might have caused. Hands were shaken all round and we were officially back in France. As we slipped away from the quay, I could almost feel the shrugging shoulders and the gesticulations in our wake.

I was anxious to get to Fumay for the Pentecost celebrations which started the following morning. We pushed on and made it worth the last lock-keeper's while to let us through his lock after closing time. He was very sympathetic when we told him that we were passionately interested in their famous cycle race which was being held the next day. This interest was a lucky invention on my part, but most villages have a bicycle race of some sort on these occasions.

Fumay is famous for its slates and must have been a big centre for barge traffic. It has a superb mooring with a wide grass lawn and the town beyond. We tied up and decided to put the dinghy in the water. This went terribly wrong: we were both very tired and neither of us had checked that the outboard was properly attached, nor that the safety rope of the motor was tied on to the dinghy. The result was that the engine ended up at the bottom of the canal. Depressed, we decided to tackle the problem in the morning.

The next morning we became the centre of attention and the chief of the fire brigade was sent for. He told us that he could get someone who knew how to use a grappling iron. This infuriated Ray who redoubled his efforts in this direction: within minutes his little anchor snagged on to the motor and he had it inboard in no time. While he got the engine going again, I went for a walk round the town to find out what was going on. There was a procession from some shrine about three kilometres away to the main church and I could hear the chanting as a statue of the Virgin was carried down the steep streets. Two naughty boys who had obviously been forced to join in were being hissed into line by a stern priest.

After some inquiries, I discovered that the main event was to be a strange race where the contestants ran for a while, then mounted their bikes and, depending on what class they were in, cycled off into the woods and hills for either eighteen or forty kilometres. This meant that it was very difficult to discover who was doing what. The first batch set off amid a good deal of incomprehensible chat on the Tannoy system, interspersed with jolly music. The second batch left just as the first lot were returning. The exhausted runners were given cups of water by pretty girls stretched out along the road and then, to my bafflement, the contestants ran to their bicycles and immediately changed their trousers, vigorously assisted by their wives and girlfriends. Once the pants were on, the cycling shoes, which had been neatly laid out, were quickly laced up and off they pedalled. The hours passed, exhausted runners came and went, cyclists returned, the running buffet got going. The prizes were displayed. There is, in France, a huge industry in manufacturing cups for sporting events such as these. In this event alone, in little Fumay, there were at least thirty trophies to be dispensed. I could see it was all going to take a very long time and returned to watch the proceedings from the barge.

The prettiest of the girls who had been dispensing the cups of cold mineral water to the runners turned out to be one of the representatives of the sponsors of the event, Citroën, and she was drafted into the job of chief trophy-giver and kisser. The casual observer can be confused by the protocol of cheek kissing in France. It would appear that in Northern France the norm is three kisses starting on the right cheek, but from Paris southwards it is four kisses, two on either cheek. By this time there was a sizable crowd picnicking on the grass by the boat. The families of the contestants cheered their men and the teams they were in, and everyone basked in the sunshine of that May afternoon in this beautiful place. Fathers took toddlers for tiny walks, holding their babies' hands above their heads to steady them; a Moroccan woman sterilized her baby's bottle by giving it a good suck before she put it in her offspring's mouth. The buffet cooked sausages and *frites* and the girls behind the counter flirted with the men of their choice. Even the police broke out a case of Orangina and smiled a bit. Gradually the crowd drifted away. As the buffet was packed up, the organizers played old-fashioned *bal musette* accordion music over the loudspeakers, and the buffet girls picked their partners and danced on the platform where the prizes had been given.

I left Fumay with a tinge of sadness. *Liberté, égalité* and *fraternité* seemed to be working admirably in this little town with its high unemployment and beautiful valley. My French is passable, and it was a real pleasure to converse with people and not be able to hear the slightest trace of class in their voices, as one does in England.

The *Leo* ploughed up through the valley of the Meuse and through the part that is called Les Dames de Meuse. Here there are three ill-defined ridges in the heavily wooded hillside which are Les Dames. They were so named after God had turned three unfaithful wives into parts of the hillside when their husbands had returned from the wars and found out what they had been up to. This ravishingly beautiful

71

stretch, or *bief* as the French call the stretch of water between two locks, is what makes the barge people dreamy when they talk about the Meuse. While their lives are undoubtedly very hard, such beauty must make them catch their breath as they pass through it: alone at the helm for hours on end, they have time for nobler thoughts than many mere workers labouring away at their allotted tasks in the daily grind. The sky was blue, the sun was hot, the country green and unspoiled; the only thing missing were ducks. Ever since we had crossed the border from Belgium into France, there had been a noticeable absence of duck families, with their proud mums taking their broods for swimming lessons. I do not think we were passing through a region with a passion for duck soup but rather through a wooded and wild part, where the foxes and other predators took their toll of these charming birds.

We stopped alongside an old barge which had been converted by a strange-looking gentleman with a long white, wispy beard and sandals, who lived there with his pretty young wife, their baby daughter and a Japanese boy. This strange group were potters, something I had not guessed when I stopped, the signs for their establishment being on the land side. Pottery is not something that I find very exciting and what they were producing fell well within the dull belt. Inside the barge, which was vast, were shelves and shelves of this firing and that, all neatly arranged in unsold rows. I felt sorry for them and desperately looked around for something I could buy that would make them feel that their endeavour was bound to succeed, when in fact it was clearly going to founder. I found a special kind of butter dish in which the butter is scraped into the lid and some water is put in the bottom of the pot. The water keeps the butter cold and therefore fresh for much longer than it would on a plate. I was very surprised to find that this device worked extremely well over the coming months, so perhaps the potters are on to a winner. Still, I somehow doubt it.

We stopped at Charleville-Mézières and I went to have a look at its famous square which had been built at the same time as the celebrated Place des Vosges in Paris. The square is large, with a colonnade around the sides full of cafés and shops. The walls of the houses are crumbling a bit and still have the peeling paint of the signs of former establishments, which I found very charming. The cafés were full and I fell into conversation with a group of kids who were pleased to be offered a coffee in exchange for a bit of local chat. I marvelled at the splendour of the square but they immediately contradicted me saying that the town was a dump and that they were dying to leave and make their fortunes in Paris. I told them that everyone wanted to go to the big city at their age, but they were adamant. They had no work, they told me, and the prospects of ever getting a regular job in their lifetime in this town were dim. They said they did not want to end up like the group of winos sitting round the base of the splendid fountain in filthy, unshaven heaps. They had just seen Michael Douglas in *Wall Street* and felt that his was the kind of life they were cut out for. I told them what I was doing and they said it was far too slow for them and they preferred to see that sort of thing on the television. Their aim was only to find a way out of Charleville-Mézières and go to the big city where it all happened. I doubt that they will ever stay away for long, but their high spirits and excitement made me start to think about being in Paris myself again soon.

Under way again, in the cool of the evening, we passed a couple from the Midlands in a steel yacht, who had decided to start a boat-hire firm on one of the canals and were looking around for a suitable site. I admired their courage and hoped inwardly that they did not find that the market was already saturated with plastic boats 'sleeping six in comfort'. How often I had seen families in these hire boats in the midst of the most magnificent countryside, with the father miserably driving, and the rest of the family watching television.

That evening we moored in a perfect sunset in the midst of fields, far from signs of habitation. We seemed to have come a great distance in a day; from being in the heart of the Ardennes to the real France. It all seemed too good to be true. The only thing that was apparently amiss was the terrific vibration on the propeller which we had first noticed in Belgium. I decided that we should be able to reach Pont-à-Bar before the famous French 'at-midday-everything-stops-for-lunch', the next day.

We reached Pont-à-Bar in good shape and went to see the chandler in this remote place, which is famous simply because it is a canal and river junction that anyone who passes up and down the waterways knows as a milestone. There was a crane there, and the man who owned it was extremely helpful and in no time the *Leo* was dangling by one of the strops we had bought in London. The crane-driver had put one strop only under the stern of the tug and had just lifted the boat a little out of the water, so that the bows were practically submerged. To show that he did not really relish putting my dear *Leo* in this extremely ungainly position, he donned a pair of completely unnecessary dark glasses. A quick glance at the propeller showed that it was indeed badly bent on the tips of the blades. A good two inches on two blades had been bent over as though some giant had twiddled it round a finger. Ray and I undid the nut that held the propeller on to the shaft by wading thigh-deep in the muddy sludge of the Pont-à-Bar canal. Taking the old propeller off and putting a new one on was a simple job – but if only I had noticed, even in those unpleasant circumstances, the little flaw that was to cause us so much trouble later in the voyage!

We were soon on our way again but I have a dreadful antipathy to Wednesday: nothing ever seems to go right for me on a Wednesday and this Wednesday was no exception. We had not gone more than a few kilometres down the canal when Ray suddenly found himself unable to stop the boat because the gear-cable control lever had snapped off. I saw him leap into the engine room and switch off the engine while I rushed to the wheel and steered the boats towards a muddy bank. We came to a rather abrupt stop, and cutlery and cups cascaded to the floor, but luckily not too much was smashed.

We managed to fix up a temporary repair, which meant having the tug floorboards up all the time; this was a real hazard and caused banged shins and stubbed toes every time I went by. We made our way to the nearest phone box and I phoned the crane-driver who said he could arrange for us to pick up a replacement cable at the next barge junction town, which in this case was to be Rheims. I felt very pleased that we had been taken for professionals and that this service of picking up spare parts from the next convenient stop had been extended to us. It required a good deal of trust on the part of the trader, but we were not going to get too far away on the canals and in any case every lock-keeper who saw us would certainly remember this ramshackle craft as it puttered through his lock.

Our next big hurdle was the flight of automatic locks at Rethel. That day we passed thirty-four locks, something of a record. A party of schoolchildren came on board for a couple of them, while their teacher explained how the automatic locks worked. As the barge entered the lock, a lever sticking out from its side was pushed back by the side of the boat, and that triggered the system for shutting the gates behind us. When one is in a smaller boat it is necessary to operate this lever by hand, otherwise the gates will not close. Once inside the lock, there are two bars, one red and one blue. The red one is for emergency; when the blue one is lifted it lets the water out of the lock (or lets it in if you are going up). Once the lock is empty, the doors open and as the boat leaves the lock another lever is pushed by the side of the vessel, and the gates, after a suitable interval, close. The children were extremely well behaved and interested and I am sure that they had a really exceptional teacher. They all left at the next lock and walked up the hill to their bikes – presumably on their way back to school.

Ray decided that he had seen too many fish jumping in the water to let them get away with it much longer, so we went into a fishing shop at the next town. Every town in France remotely near water has a fishing-tackle shop, as fishing is without any question the most popular sport in France. Why the French sit for hours watching floats in muddy water, to try to catch fish which are at best less than tasty, is very hard to understand, but I suppose it must have enormous fascination. The first really warm days of summer were upon us and the fishing enthusiasts were already perched on the banks and getting their invective ready for the innocent British barge that would pass by and destroy the moment when that monster of the deep was about to swallow their bait. I translated for Ray as he purchased what the man in the shop told us was the bait of the season: red worms, which he produced live from his fridge. We would have no problems, he said. I was sure that the fish would have no problems either.

I recalled an occasion when my son Jason had been taken with the fishing bug on the Canal du Centre many years before, and had bought a box of white maggots in similar circumstances. He had left them open on the hatch above the pillow on my bunk. During the night a gust of wind had blown the plastic pot over so that all the maggots had fallen on to my head. When I awoke in the morning, I thought for one dreadful moment that I was dead and in my grave as I felt those disgusting creatures creeping over my skin.

I put up part of the canopy to get a spot of shade, as the steel deck was beginning to get very hot during the afternoons. We stopped early that evening because Ray wanted to try his hand at fishing. Neither of us were sure what the local rules about fishing were, so we chose a spot where we would be unseen except by some sheep. We might just as well not have concerned ourselves about the niceties of permissions, for Ray sat for hours watching his lifeless float until he was forced inside by an enormous cloudburst after a dramatic electrical storm. I made sure the red worms were safely sealed on deck!

The other traffic on the canal was very slight. We had passed two laden barges under way with fertilizer and a British yacht called *Contented Lady*. The woman in question stood on the minuscule deck sipping a gin and tonic while her husband steered, contentment oozing from every pore as she peered down her nose at us – clearly not members of the white-plimsoll yachting fraternity. There is nothing so frigid as the British greeting each other in places where they think that only they, or their class of people, should be.

Berry-au-Bac is another waterway junction that everyone on the water knows. We arrived there in the evening in the pouring rain with nothing left in the larder. I made an impassioned plea for something to eat and the *éclusière* came up trumps with a live chicken and some champagne of excellent quality for a mere fifty-two francs a bottle. I suppose it must have fallen off the back of a barge somewhere. I took the chicken back to the barge, holding it by the string that the woman had tied round its ankles, wondering if I could remember how to cope with the execution and plucking. To my surprise and relief, Ray announced that when he had started his working life he had been a butcher's boy and the situation held no fears for him at all. And so it was that we had roast chicken and champagne that rainy evening in Berry-au-Bac. Tomorrow we would be in the heart of champagne-country in Rheims.

It rained all night and all the next day as we steamed on to Rheims. I could never have guessed, as we moored in the centre, that this great city was to throw up the surprise that it did. I wanted to see the room where the Germans and the Allies had signed the Armistice at the end of the Second World War. When I got there I found the Armistice Room

77

full of men and women in battle fatigues. For a moment I took no notice, but then I wondered what on earth these people were doing there, and I asked them what they were up to. I was told that they were a group of military vehicle enthusiasts who collected Second World War vehicles for a hobby, and that they had come to this part of the country to attend a huge rally of like-minded loonies at Mourmelon the next day. They invited me to come along to see their pride and joy, an American ambulance, apparently authentic in every way. One of their party had gone to the trouble of buying an equally authentic pack of Lucky Strike, and had stuck it in the netting over his US GI-type tin helmet.

Mourmelon is a huge area reserved for military manoeuvres by the French army, with a small garrison-town in the midst of it. The public had been allowed in for this vast meeting of military freaks. It was an excuse for dressing up, which I suppose is something the French take to, but on a scale and with a seriousness I had never seen before. I spoke to a giant of a man dressed as a Scottish soldier, from a regiment, he explained, that had been raised from Scottish settlers in Charleston on the Ohio River to fight the Yankees. There were groups of French pretending to be GIs and singing American marching songs with a French accent. There were men dressed up as the French army in the trenches at Verdun. All types of settlers from the Midwest of America mingled with Zouaves and other glamorous sections of the historical French armies. In the midst of this strange gathering were the French national servicemen who had been drafted to shepherd these garish crowds into the right sections of the encampment. I asked one of them whether, when his time was up, he would dress up and come to one of these rallies. 'Certainly not,' he replied, 'I'm no Fascist.'

In a far corner of this foreign field was a small encampment of people dressed up as Royal Army Service Corps soldiers. Their leader, a young Englishman dressed as a Lieutenant, told me he was the barman at the British Legion in Paris, and

The Dames de Meuse in the Ardennes.

A holiday Sunday, Fumay.

The Pont des Arts, Paris.

explained that they had chosen the RASC because it was the only unit for which they could get all the insignia. He was enormously proud of his efforts, which were indeed splendid, and had gathered round him a group of Frenchmen who were delightedly digging trenches and playing with Vickers machine guns. I suppose that this kind of activity was the highlight of their season but it all seemed to me to represent a great deal of misspent energy. I mentioned to him that I had just seen a Frenchman dressed as a British Field Marshal wearing the Victoria Cross, and asked him what the form was about this sort of medal abuse. He told me that he would kill anyone insulting such orders. Put to the test minutes later, he only managed to persuade the Field Marshal, who insolently never removed a drooping Gauloise from his lips while speaking, to cover up the offending ribbon. I felt really quite sorry for him in the midst of this stupid charade, as he explained to the Frenchman that his father had fought to get some of the other medals on his chest. The Frenchman's attitude was that he had such a high regard for the British Army that he felt quite justified in wearing these medal ribbons. I think if the truth were known he probably thought the colours of the ribbons suited his sallow complexion.

CHAPTER FIVE

Rheims to Paris

Rheims is the commercial heart of the Champagne district. The low rolling hills with their chalky soil make it ideal for growing just the right grape for the wine that is used in Dom Perignon's famous invention, and, perhaps most importantly, the ground is ideal for tunnelling enormous caves to store the precious liquid for the required period. Everywhere tourist trips are advertised for visits to the establishments of the famous champagne houses, so, ever curious, I went along to try to find the answer to something that had always puzzled me. Everyone knows that champagne comes from this district alone and the growers from this part of the world spend fortunes on defending the name so that other manufacturers in other parts of the world are not able to sell their products calling it champagne. Since the number of hectares available for cultivation is finite, how was it that every year another few million bottles of champagne are produced?

I decided on a company with a German name and had the regular tour with a charming lady whose deliciously accented English somehow added to the mystery, as she spoke of the 'distinguished bubbles' her company produced. We tramped through the vast underground labyrinths these places possess. I had the feeling of being in a James Bond film, as small electrical tractors rushed around with grim-looking drivers, unaware of the world, their heads swathed under enormous ear-protectors. The process that Dom Perignon invented has been scientifically refined for better, faster production but the principles remain the same. Rival houses have even contested the claim that the Dom actually invented champagne and claim it was a process that was already well advanced when he made it famous. This he did by using doses of it to cure the remorse, during confession, of a certain loose-living countess. She subsequently introduced it to the Court of Louis XIV, and so made both the wine and the Dom famous.

It became clear on our tour that, however the wine was made, the greatest factor in its rise to stardom was the enormous amount of energy that went into the business of selling it to the public. The company I went to had kept all their nineteenth-century posters and advertisements which were fascinating. A particularly striking poster of a girl in a bright yellow skirt, sitting astride a bottle of bubbly which was propelling her like a rocket into the twentieth century, caught my eye. Though I could not get anyone to admit it, the wine from the famous Champagne district is blended every year with more and more wine from outside the district. I am sure that any knowledgeable wine merchant would be able to advise on what blends were closest to the contents of the bottle the girl in the yellow skirt was so sinuously clasping between her thighs. The popping of champagne corks must surely rank as one of the most deliciously anticipatory sounds in history, so very much more glamorous than the unpeeling of Velcro which has been described as the sexiest sound of the eighties.

Because of the vast public relations efforts that have been going on for so long in this part of France, it is very difficult to establish which stories are true and which are the product of some clever copywriter's imagination. I particularly liked the story that the Germans would not advance through the district during the First World War, because they had heard rumours that great numbers of French troops were hidden in the champagne cellars under the no-man's-land between the lines. The idea was that if the Germans advanced, the French would pop up as soon as they had moved forward and attack them from the rear – encouraged, no doubt, by what they had found down below.

I took a moment in the magnificent cathedral in Rheims to gaze at the superb stained glass and remember my friend Nino Rota, whose death I had heard of when I was in this city many years before. If you are very lucky in life, you may meet a genius, and Nino was the one I met. He was, of course, famous for writing practically all the music for the films of Federico Fellini and virtually creating the sound of Italy on film for many millions of people north and west of the Alps. I had met him in Rome some twenty years back while we were making *Romeo and Juliet* with Franco Zeffirelli, when he had written the famous theme for that film which now haunts me as it has become muzak in most of the lifts and airports of the world. Nino, like most Italians, was a great traveller and had visited almost every part of the world. He bought postcards wherever he went which he never posted, except through the slot in the top of the trunk that he kept in the hall of his house for that purpose. I have often wondered what happened to that trunk which must contain the most extraordinary collection of cards. His great ambition was to have an oratorio which he composed for ten thousand voices sung in the hills round Rimini – a dream which, I am happy to say, he achieved shortly before his death. To have the ability to hear music when looking at the notes on a page is something that fills me with great admiration, but to be able to compose a hit tune for one famous Italian film and then have equal success with the same tune written in reverse in another successful film, as Nino did, is quite beyond my comprehension.

Ray remarked when I got back to the barge that there was a lot of traffic coming up the canal in the opposite direction to the way that we were going: was there something we didn't know? This turned out to be very perspicacious of him as it very soon emerged, after a few inquiries, that a barge had crashed into a lock gate quite near Paris, where we were

heading along the River Marne. One of the most depressing
things when travelling is to have to turn around when one's
route is blocked, but having to turn round in a canal is
particularly depressing, especially as, if I had asked the lady
who sold us the live chicken at Berry-au-Bac, she could
probably have told us. I reminded myself always to ask, in
future, whether there were any blockages on the route ahead.
Most lock-keepers have never been up their canals and probably don't know the countryside the other side of the nearest
big town. Of course some of the lock-keepers are retired
bateliers, who, as fellow *mariniers*, always pass on any vital
scraps of information which might be of use on the
voyage.

We retraced our way to Berry-au-Bac, waving a cautionary
finger at the lady who had not told us about the closure on
the Marne, but since I had not told her where we were bound
it was not her fault in any way. She probably took it as a
friendly gesture for there was a good deal of smiling and
shrugging of shoulders. The Canal Lateral de l'Aisne brought
us to Soissons, a pleasant town for those afloat, with a fine
quay right in the centre. We arrived at the town just after
passing beneath a bridge that Joan of Arc is supposed to have
crossed. As we finished mooring, an elderly gentleman came
up to us and told us that his ninety-two-year-old mother had
become very excited because our boat was called the *Leontyne*,
which was her name, and she had never seen a boat with
that name in all her life of looking out of the window at the
River Aisne. Deeply honoured I bought her a bunch of
flowers, but when I came to deliver them, I could get no
reply from the door where her son said they lived. They
probably bolted the door early and retired to the television.

The next morning we left really early and had not gone
more than a few hundred yards when the engine's usual
regular, reliable throb suddenly spluttered to a halt. The
unforgivable had occurred; we had run out of diesel. There
is a strong current on that stretch of the Aisne and we had

to drop the anchor quickly. As the current was coming up our stern, the barge slowly swung round to face into the stream, and when we were settled we started the process of pumping fuel out of the tanks on the barge. These were very large and supplied the generator and the fuel for the Perkins cooker which is the maritime equivalent of the Aga cooker. It produced hot water, cooking facilities and a focus in the saloon which kept us warm and, above all, dry. It was not long before the Gardner engine, the best there is for maritime purposes of our sort, came to life again and we were ready to set off.

Unfortunately, as we had dropped the anchor we had drifted downstream, and now had reached a part of the river where it was too narrow to swing round under our own steam. We had no choice but to go astern (which was something that the sixty-three-year-old *Leo* was very bad at) until we reached a disused wharf where we made fast and had some breakfast. Ray had decided that the best way to get out of our predicament was to swing the barge, which in any normal circumstances is a fairly simple procedure. We tied a rope from the stern of the barge on to a bollard and then let the current swing us round. The idea was that at the crucial moment, Ray would flick off the line that was attached to the wharf and we would head sideways into the cut on the other side of the stream, which led into the next lock.

In a matter of seconds, a number of most unfortunate events occurred. Just as Ray was about to flick off the rope a large barge came hurtling downstream and started to blow at us frantically. There was just time to complete our manoeuvre but unfortunately Ray couldn't get his line off, and so there was nothing to do but tie the rope to the stern of the tug again and go ahead, so that we went back to our original position – thus avoiding the leviathan that was bearing down on us. In the excitement of getting out of the way of the barge, we had both forgotten that we had moved the dinghy to the other side of the barge and now as we swung towards

84

the quay, it was obvious that the dinghy was going to be crushed by the weight of the barge hitting the wall. Ray rushed up and succeeded in moving the dinghy forward but he was not able to avert the inevitable crunch. Luckily, the dinghy, which was a solid fibreglass dory, survived – although I have a flash-frame image in my mind of the moment of impact when the dinghy seemed to bend in half and then spring back again. Because we were now back to square one, we picked ourselves up and started all over again. Second time round, we succeeded.

In these days of voyaging, Ray and I were under way for upwards of twelve hours a day so that we could keep up to our schedule of getting to Vienna before the winter set in. The locks opened at 6.30 a.m. and closed at 7.30 p.m. with a flexible break at midday depending on the type of canal; the busy ones kept going all day, and on the Seine it was possible to travel at night for an extra charge. For us it was all free, except for the *pourboire* to the *éclusier*, which was not obligatory. The trick to speedy progress was to arrive at a lock just before it closed for the night and go through it. Then one could cover the stretch to the next lock that evening, where we would wait till morning for the lock to open. This usually meant making contact with the keeper of the lock where we intended to pass the night to tell him of our intentions. These evening chats were sometimes very amusing and sometimes downright dangerous, when guard dogs on extremely long chains would wait unseen till one was in their arc of attack, and then spring, gnashing their teeth and showing incipient signs of rabies. As a child in India, I had been bitten by a dog of questionable background, and had to have fourteen painful anti-rabies injections in the stomach. Since that time I have been extremely cautious of man's faithful friends.

When morning came, breakfast would consist of coffee

with honey and a running snack till midday when we would stop, if we could, for a meal of some sort – usually on the boat but sometimes in a café if there was one near the bank. In this way, providing there were not too many locks, we could cover about eighty kilometres a day. At the end of a day like this, there was no need whatsoever for sleeping pills.

I could tell that we were approaching Paris when, in Pontoise, I saw the first Vietnamese restaurant – a sure sign that we were close to a big city. We passed down the Oise and came to the barge capital of France, Conflans-Ste-Honorine, which lies at the junction of the Oise and the River Seine. Conflans has always been a favourite place of mine. The row upon row of barges moored there, with their brightly coloured bows and flags, are sadly increasing every time that I go. The barge people who used, when they retired, to be able to afford a little bungalow somewhere they had selected on their ceaseless roaming, were now, because of the decline of traffic on the waterways, only able to afford to live on their barges.

A complete barge community has been built up, even to the extent of having a chapel on a huge concrete barge called *Je Sers*. Père Duvallier is a massive priest of about sixty, who spends most of his days in a boilersuit helping his elderly parishioners to replace empty Calor-gas bottles, or mending generators for those who are not lucky enough to be positioned where they can get electricity from the town's supply. This splendid priest told me of his voyages as a young man, and in particular about the Danube and all its hazards. It was he who first made me realize that the horrors of the Rhine would be nothing to those we would encounter on the Danube. As we stood beside the map of the waterways of Europe, he pointed out how the French government's transport policies, ruled since the war by the railway and road lobbies, have isolated Paris from the rest of Europe as far as waterways for the now nearly standard 1300-ton barge are concerned. In the heyday of the French waterway system, the late nineteenth century, a French official called Freycinet had standardized the lock measurements so that a 350-ton barge could pass anywhere. Now the canals approaching Paris from the north and south were woefully small by modern standards and it was becoming harder and harder for the one-family-one-barge outfits to win freight away from their competitors on the railways and the roads. There *was* work but it usually meant waiting for at least fourteen days before they got another cargo.

In the stern of the church-barge, the ladies of the barge fraternity were having a jumble sale, and one of them told me about the graze on the side of the Padre's face. He had caught a couple of louts trying to break into his church and given them a hiding such as they would never forget. He never told the police, of course.

The Padre told me to go to talk to Monsieur Noisette at the *Bureau d'Affrètement* to learn about the freight system on the French canals. M. Noisette was a small, intelligent and surprisingly young man who explained very clearly how it all worked. When a barge was unloaded it was allowed to put its name on the list waiting for a further cargo. Three times a week in a special hall (which looked a bit like the room where the bookmakers call over the prices of horses in the Classic races on the British Turf), the barge fraternity would gather to have a good grouse about how hard things were. The names of the barges would be called out and the captains would come forward and accept the freight, or they would pass and let someone else have it if they did not want to go to that destination. They did not lose their place in the queue for the next callover.

Freight rates are fixed by the various associations involved throughout France, representing the *bateliers*, the people who wanted their freight transported, and the government. To even things out, a ton of something very voluminous has a higher freight rate than a ton of sand and gravel.

The position with barges from another country is more complicated. A Belgian barge, for instance, can only take a cargo back to Belgium, and not take freight to another part of France. I must say I doubt very much whether this sort of restriction will change in 1992 when all these rules are meant to be swept away. It seems unlikely, for example, that Ray will be able to take a cargo in a British barge from one side of France to another.

Many of the *bateliers* have, in recent years, turned their barges into pusher barges with dumb barges at the front, like one of the *bateliers* whom I met in Conflans, M. Ollivier of the *Baikal*. This allows them to take bigger cargoes, but it limits where they can go because they cannot fit into one of M. Freycinet's smaller locks. I went to visit the *Baikal* which had been laid up in the shipyard because Ollivier had struck a floating tree and smashed his propeller, which was now being changed. He had met his pretty wife on the canals and they had done what many courting couples amongst the *batelier* families do: they had scribbled secret messages on the lock gates whilst waiting for the locks to fill up. Barge families tend to stick together, with families marrying into each other and fathers leaving their barges to sons-in-law they approve of. The women have as much to do with navigation and generally running the boat as the men nowadays. In some cases I have seen whole crews made up of women, but they must be pretty tough because there is inevitably a lot of heavy work to be done, from time to time.

Mme Ollivier had told me that, for her wedding, her parents had looked about for a friend's barge which had been recently transporting flour. The residue of white dust inside the hold had given a suitably bridal aura, and a tradition had been extended for another generation. 'Today,' she told me, 'it would be much more difficult to find such a barge, because flour is transported by road and rail.'

Weddings are very important to barge people, and a certain M. Chantre told me of how his parents had made arches of roses up the gangway for the bride to walk through. M. Chantre is the grand old man of the *batelier* world and had known that I would knock on his door: I suspect that there was very little that went on on the river that he did not know about. He has written books about his life on the waterways and he paints a great deal, mostly in oils. One of the lasting images that all voyagers have is of the great piles that are driven into the sides of the rivers, away from the banks, for barges to moor against while they are waiting for a lock to open. Usually, when the *batelier* gets up in the morning, these are the first things that he sees, and that is why they are called *'les ducs de l'aube'*, the dukes of the dawn. M. Chantre had included these in most of his evocative paintings which he proudly showed me in the minuscule studio at the back of his council flat in Conflans. He told me that there were many poets amongst his colleagues because barge people are very often alone in the midst of nature and have time to think grand thoughts. He also told me proudly that his feet did not touch *terra firma* till he was fifteen days old. He had been born in Le Havre and his brother had been born in the south, at Sète. His grandparents had been buried where they died, so his family had been dotted all over France, but nowadays, with refrigeration, everyone came home to Conflans. Sainte Honorine herself had been martyred in Le Havre at the mouth of the Seine and the monks had brought her bones to Conflans by barge.

He told me stories for hours about the old days on the canals, of how in the Bourgogne, where I planned to go, the *bateliers* would have a complicated double act which they performed with great skill. The area fifty metres either side of a lock is generally regarded as being in the gift of the lock-keeper, and therefore the fishing belongs to them. The best place to catch fish on a canal is close to a lock because that is where the best food supplies are, so while their barge went through, one of the *bateliers* would get on to the bank and engage the lock-keeper in some enthralling story which kept his mind off what was happening in the lock, where the other *batelier* was busily hauling in his net full of fish.

In those days, before the internal combustion engine, the barges were either drawn by man or donkey. Horses were only used on the bigger rivers where there was a land-based service for hauling barges. This was because the *bateliers* had to take their animals with them when they drifted down the bigger rivers, and they could not fit horses very easily into their barges. During M. Chantre's tales I began to realize how fiercely independent the barge people were, and how proud they were of their *métier*. Something that struck me very strongly when I got to France was the tremendous pride people had in their jobs: they did not have the attitude that seems to prevail in the UK where people decry what they do as a necessary evil forced on them between sessions of watching television.

Conflans is built on a spur, and on the top is a fine nineteenth-century merchant's house, that has been turned into a museum of barges. Barges are one of the oldest types of transport and this museum has some fine models, but what interested me most was the development of the one-time barge. On the Dordogne in south-western France, the bargemen would build a wooden raft in the bed of the river and wait for the rains to come and sweep the barge and them down to the sea. Here they would unload their cargoes and sell the timber from which the raft was made for building materials. This technique was incredibly dangerous and there were many accidents: it must have been a bit like shooting the rapids in a 300-ton inflatable boat. Some of these French daredevils started a very good business on the Mississippi, building rafts in Tennessee and floating them down to Natchez. Many of the buildings on the foreshore today are built with the timbers from these rafts. On their way home they walked up a path called the Natchez trail which has been brilliantly preserved by the US government.

Conflans has many things to recommend it; one is the

excellent collection of *charcutiers*: I suppose that delicious snacks for the journey must be something that any good French *batelier* would go a long way to find. Another is a really excellent chandler, who sells serious gadgets for barges and little mini items for plastic boats. I decided to treat the *Leo* to an enormous chrome foghorn called a 'Super Boeuf', so named because it had an air compressor which gave its voice the requisite lowing quality. I wanted the *Leo* to sound serious, even if she did look a bit odd.

We were moored on the very tip of the junction of the Oise and the Seine where, day and night, huge barges would skilfully take the sharp corner and float round with the current. They always show their blue signs when doing this because it is impossible for them to pass oncoming traffic port side to port side, which is the norm. The largest vessel that I saw on this stretch of the Seine was the Renault car-delivery ship which takes upwards of five hundred cars from one Renault plant to another up and down the Seine. These ships look enormous when they are coming straight towards you, and you imagine that the helmsman cannot see you, but he is actually able to raise and lower his entire wheelhouse hydraulically, and have a good look.

The big barges that go up and down the Seine these days are on such a tight schedule that they have to be refuelled while they pass up the main water street of Conflans. Jean-Michel and his uncle have started an enterprising service with their tanker barge, the *Piranha*. They supply fuel and water and all those other requirements like bottled gas for cooking and the inevitable crate of beer. Channel 12 on the VHF is forever crackling with demands for the *Piranha* to stand by and service the barges as they come through; all spoken in the most impenetrable *argot* of the *batelier*. Jean-Michel had heard of our impending arrival in Conflans long before we got there. The bush telegraph on the waterways is extremely effective, and woe betide anyone who tries to get away without paying a bill. On all my voyages I have often left my boat unlocked for long periods in France, and I have never had anything stolen.

We left Conflans on the first of June, refreshed by the contact with the professional world of the river – but I had been saddened to see how much the traffic had declined since I was there last. The Seine meanders its way into Paris in great loops. The banks are lined with bungalows and then quite suddenly the bungalows give way to a gravel tip or a race-course. As we approached Paris we came to a suburb at a place called Châtou where there's a little island in the middle of the river which is famous for the Maison Fournier. Alphonse Fournier was a boatman who hired out day boats for people to row on the Seine. His business blossomed when the railway put his establishment within reach of the daytrippers from the big city. He soon started a restaurant and, blessed with a beautiful daughter and a practical son, became very successful with the writers and painters of the day.

We moored at the old quay outside an isolated house which was in the process of being repaired by a conservation group from Châtou, led by Henrietta Claudel – whose husband was once France's Ambassador to Washington. As we wandered round, a charming and urbane diplomat arrived to check on how the repairs were progressing, and was soon telling us of all the painters and writers that had sat on the balcony a century or so ago. Renoir painted some of his most famous pictures there, Maupassant kept a room in the attic, Monet, Manet and the rest of that famous group all used to catch the train to Châtou on a Sunday. They liked the light, the girls and Alphonse Fournier, who was very kind to the penniless artists. His daughter, economically named Alphonsine, figures in Renoir's painting *The Boating Party*, as does his son, also called Alphonse. No wonder an A was woven into the wrought-iron design of the famous balcony.

The house itself had fallen into disrepair and had been squatted by many Algerian families until the conservationists of Châtou decided to repair it, and start a restaurant there once more. The Claudels kindly gave us a very good meal which Mme Claudel had prepared herself in their beautiful house at Châtou, bought by M. Claudel's famous playwright father from the family who had built it in 1634. His aunt was the famous sculptress Camille Claudel, who had such a torridly tortuous affair with Rodin. Now the second generation were restoring the house where penniless young painters had sponged on Fournier for a meal and a little fresh air. I wonder whether there was an impressionist amongst the Algerian squatters who were thrown out.

There is, at times, a three- or four-knot current in the Seine from Conflans up to Paris – a journey of some seventy kilometres because of the enormous bends in the river. In the 1840s a heavy chain was laid on the bed of the river, to which a barge with a motorized capstan was attached. This device was able to tow fifteen laden barges at the same time up to Paris. The motor of this contraption was driven by a small, forty-horsepower steam turbine, which was, by today's standards, incredibly efficient: the normal Freycinet 350-ton barges require at least 250 horsepower to push them up against the Seine's current to Paris.

Given the loops, it would take us a while to reach Paris from Conflans, even though as the crow flies it's practically inside the city. That night we stopped near Sèvres because I had always wanted to see what the famed *manufacture* was like. There is a museum, at this world-renowned porcelain factory, full of rather monumental objects, which I suppose is great if you are the head of state somewhere and have a need for suitably grandiose urns in your hallway. Behind the museum it becomes more interesting. Here, there are a great number of double-storey eighteenth-century buildings where the work is done in large, airy workshops with huge windows. Everything is covered with a very fine, powdery dust from the porcelain, which has a most pleasing effect on the red-brick floors.

The great secret of the porcelain manufacturers is the way they decorate their wares. It is not a closely guarded secret, but simply something that requires a very considerable amount of experience of what happens to the colours on the china when it is put in the kilns. The most important part of any apprentice's examination is getting his palette correct. He has to know what the effect of the various kilns will be on these discs of china which are painted with little squares of shaded colour. The very hot firings can take as much as ten days, the cooler ones five, so there must be a lot of angst while an object that may have taken months to paint is locked away in the kiln. The kilns are brick, banded by huge metal straps, and until very recently heated by oak logs. They look like giant beehives and are built inside the main structure of the factory, which keeps everything dry in the winter.

The French government own and subsidize this model of enlightened factory building, and I had a very strong feeling of an established group isolated from the outside world. In return for cocooning these talented people, the government is able to have the plates missing from the Sèvres services belonging to friendly despots replaced. These patient experts have been painting spring flowers from one generation to the next, never writing down the steps they take, but rather working with an apprentice till he (or she) is ready to start on his own. Probably the thing that impressed me most in this fascinating place was the engraver who was doing a design for the bicentennial of the French Revolution, using a design which he had just been to collect from the archives of 1793. I very much doubt whether any upheaval in the outside world makes the slightest difference to this Shangri-la in the suburbs of Paris. I watched a girl with red hair and pretty ankles climb a ladder in the paint store to collect a jar of powder that had been mixed in 1906. When I asked what she painted at the weekend, after five days of flowers, she replied sweetly that she painted more flowers. She said she liked flowers.

When I got back to the boat, I found Ray, who had stayed there to wait for an electrician to arrive, having a fierce argument with the man. Ray did not speak French and the electrician, who was installing an electrical supply for the Super Boeuf, spoke no English. The electrician had brought his teenage nephew along to assist him, however; the boy was acting as the go-between, and, I suspect, slanting the translation to favour his irascible uncle's position. The electrician had told Ray that he thought that the British Navy had just been lucky and were really not all they were cracked up to be; the French on the other hand were tactically superior. He had read a great deal on this subject and we were no match for him, except that from our insular point of view all that he was saying was clearly tosh.

I reminded Ray of his colleague Reggie on the Thames who had a passion for geographical place names, pointing out that this man was of a similar type: we would never persuade him that his point of view was simply not correct. I suggested to Ray that he make a cup of British tea all round, hoping that this would not provoke another argument about the origin and superiority of various forms of tea. Later, with a hot mugful cooling his temper, the electrician demonstrated his work, and the Super Boeuf bellowed satisfactorily. He certainly knew his negative from his positive, even if he was not so hot on his history.

That night we moored at Port Levallois which has a very large Algerian population. The bars were full of dangerous-looking men, with flashing gold teeth and brilliantined hair, their women discreetly apart and dressed for some kind of Arabian *Come Dancing* festival. Ray and I had a beer and were eyed with a great deal of suspicion while we drank. We were the only Northern Europeans in this crowded bar: I had forgotten how much Paris is split up into its *quartiers*. Many people I know feel very strange outside their own little world in Paris, and I suppose the same is true of London. Cab drivers have often cautioned me, when I have taken a cab home to Rotherhithe, that I had better look out down there because the place is only inhabited by rogues and villains.

After a little shopping in the garish Arab shops, we clambered back over an enormous barge which a wiry lady psychiatrist appeared to be converting single-handed. She had moored her barge on the right bank of the river because during the floods of the previous winter, the water level had risen so much that her barge had been in danger of being marooned on the towpath like a huge beached whale. The flood water rises quite alarmingly quickly on the Seine and, these days, almost always catches the houseboat population unawares, as many of the barges are owned by well-heeled jetsetters who leave them unattended while on holiday in the sun. I had an animated conversation with the psychiatrist's daughter who had just taken her finals in medicine and was very keen to go on to a career in medical research. She had a revulsion for actually coming into contact with the sick, which I found very odd. She said that she felt she could honour her Hippocratic oath perfectly well without laying hands on live patients, and I suppose in today's medicine it is a very good thing that there are people who only want to work in laboratories.

The morning that we entered Paris was brilliant. As we chugged up the river past the Bois de Boulogne, we saw a display of the most fanciful houseboats and floating restaurants. Designers and individualists have had a field day with some of these hulls; it would be too much to call them boats. There are men-of-war from the eighteenth century, enormous modern gravel barges converted into palaces with swimming pools, even a submarine's conning-tower section with the end cut off. On the other side of these strange craft, I could see the cars slowing to have a closer look at the girls parading themselves for custom along the edge of the Bois de Boulogne. Then suddenly, over the trees, we saw the Eiffel Tower – that everlasting symbol of Paris – towering over the city like a great giraffe. We had arrived.

CHAPTER SIX

Paris

Arriving in the heart of Paris by river after a journey of six weeks must surely be one of the most exciting things that I have ever done. By the time we had passed the Eiffel Tower, the sun was already setting and there was a golden glow on the Pont Alexandre III. All the familiar buildings were, somehow surprisingly, still there. I could see the obelisk in the Place de la Concorde, the Louvre, the Gare d'Orsay (now a museum). Behind the *Leo* the sun was shining through the glass roof of the Grand Palais, making it look as though it were on fire. The last determined sunbathers were rolling up their towels on the *quais*, lights from the pleasure boats, or *bateaux mouches*, were starting to pick out the stonework under the arches, and everywhere was the unique sound of Parisian traffic which, from the river, was reduced to a muffled roar.

I was rather anxious about where to moor. It is usually possible to find a mooring on the rivers of France, but here we were in the capital, and though I did not have any clear idea where I could tie up, I did know where I wanted to. I have always been very fond of the Pont des Arts, a footbridge which crosses the Seine from the Louvre to the bottom of the Rue de Seine on the Left Bank. The bridge, which has been recently rebuilt after a barge smashed one of its piers, is just where I like to be in Paris. As luck would have it there was a space right underneath the bridge itself, alongside some neat sandstone steps. When we had tied up I remember Ray went to the stern of the *Leo* and just sat and watched the last moments of the sunset. I sat on the hatch on the barge and wondered how it was that I had been lucky enough to fetch up in a place like this.

Ray was leaving the boat in the morning for a few days with his girl in an hotel, so I left him to go for a walk round *la rive gauche*. I crossed the *quai*, walked up the Rue de Seine, and peered into the shops. On my way I passed the house at No. 1 where my friend Louis Fleury lived in his prime, when he was the man to whom all American and English film companies went if they wanted to make films in France.

Fleury arranged permissions and that sort of thing, but he was an unofficial ambassador for France. A huge man with enormous charm, it was quite impossible to get down to the boring part of business with him because he was always recounting some amusing incident on a film he had handled. The polish with which he could handle the cross executive who had just flown the Atlantic to get to the bottom of a financial matter from a past film location was wonderful to see. His apartment was in a house which belonged to the Ville de Paris and he paid very little rent but had furnished it well. He had a wife who always kept in the background on these occasions in the upstairs kitchen. When the visiting fireman panted to the top of the stairs, Louis would begin his performance by offering a cup of hot *bouillon* which was probably the very last thing the visitor expected. I do not know what was in that soup but I remember watching it calm the angry, get-to-the-bottom-of-it-all type many times. Because the soup was hot and served in a drinking bowl its consumption required a lot of concentration, and this was when Louis started his solo. I never saw him fail: whatever the financial outrages from the past, they were polished away with the ease and speed of a professional waiter wiping the table tops outside a Parisian café.

A few doors further up the street, I passed the house where the English bookshop had been. It was run by the Olympia Press and was famous for selling books banned at that time in Britain, like D. H. Lawrence's *Lady Chatterley's Lover* or Henry Miller's *Tropic of Cancer*, and, for the less literary-minded who had strayed into the tiny shop, straight porno-graphic novels. It was here that I first met a man who has since become one of London's leading film critics, but at that time was penniless in Paris and making ends meet by writing these steamy novels for the Olympia Press. I remember asking him what it was like to have to write blue books. He said that the sheer repetitiousness of the sexual act, and the need to have a torrid scene every two or three pages to warm the readers up, was what got him down.

Paris is a city that seems to renew itself from time to time in the most dramatic ways. Haussmann, in the nineteenth century, tore out the heart of the medieval city and replaced it with the great boulevards everyone knows today. In the 1970s Les Halles, the romantic food markets, were destroyed and replaced by one of the most offensive buildings in the Western world. The reasons for this destruction were re-ported to be traffic problems and vermin in the old markets. The traffic problems have not been improved and the vermin in the myriad restaurants that have sprung up in their place literally live off the fat of the land. The Left Bank, apart from the monstrous Tour de Montparnasse, has been renewed in another way which is more insidious. All the character that made it the intellectual heart of the city has been eroded by expensive shops and tourists who have come to experience the Paris of Hemingway; but behind the great doors of the houses on the boulevards there are still sleepy courtyards which have a whiff of the old Paris.

As I walked I wondered why I liked this city so much. The first time I had gone to Paris as a very young man I can remember being more lonely there than at any other time in my life. I had flown there in the fifties for a holiday after a long location in a dismal part of the world. I made all the tourist trips but, knowing no one in Paris, I decided to return to London earlier than I had planned. In those days, when there was bad weather, air passengers were sent back to London on a train – and first class at that. In the corner of my compartment was a *soignée* middle-aged woman, who for no apparent reason told me why she was going to London. She had been a nurse for the Free French Forces in Cairo during the war and had fallen madly in love with a handsome British officer. A *coup de foudre*, she said, and she told me of the romance of the pyramids in the moonlight as we rattled through the valley of the Somme.

I was wondering where this conversation was leading when she told me that she had met the same Englishman at a party in Paris a few years before and, though both were married, they'd started an affair, perhaps meeting once a year. She was travelling to London for a rendezvous which, they had planned, was to decide whether they were going to leave their respective spouses and go off together. He was leaving for the States that evening and they were to have had the day together to decide whether she would simply leave with him, but the fog had put an end to all that. While I had trundled round the world quite a lot for a 23-year-old, I found this story very French, immensely grown-up and therefore fascinating. I made her promise to let me know how things ended for her in London. As I had suspected it ended badly: he had left a huge bunch of flowers in her hotel room with a note telling her that he could not leave his wife and had gone off to America alone. She went back to her scientist husband, and I felt I had a friend in Paris: from that moment I have always loved the city. It was like seeing that answering flash in a woman's eyes, when you decide whether you are going to like each other or not.

Mornings in Paris in June are a wonderful time. I bought a croissant for the gentleman of the road, or *clochard*, who was sleeping under the Pont des Arts alongside the boat. When he woke, I gave him a cup of coffee and asked him about his life. I had half expected some philosopher of the road but he was more concerned with minutiae of his day-today existence. He had been on the road sleeping rough for eight years (twelve years is about the average time for sleeping rough, after which the bronchitis kills). He had started when he was twenty when, as the eldest of eight children, he had left his widowed mother in Strasbourg unable, he said, to face the responsibility. Friday morning was the time to avoid under the Pont des Arts, he told me, because the authorities washed the slatted walkways on the bridge above and any gentlemen of the road got a thorough soaking if they were sleeping below. He managed to get by from day to day by helping load and unload in the market at the top of the Rue de Seine, and it had made him enough to be really quite smartly dressed, which he said was essential for keeping out of the clutches of the police who were always searching his colleagues for drugs. He clearly had quite serious problems with his chest and wheezed and coughed all the time I spoke with him. When I asked him why he did not get himself fixed up with a room somewhere, he pointed to the Seine in the beautiful morning light, which had pulled a fine theatrical gauze over the river and the city, and asked where he could find a room with a view like this.

I saw that he had a copy of 'Tintin' which was his favourite reading, and he told me how much he liked Milou the dog. I asked him why and he told me it was because Milou never shat. One of the great problems of riparian life in any city is that river walkways are a favourite place for people to take their dogs to evacuate themselves, and consequently they are over-endowed with droppings. I do not think he liked dogs much: I suppose that they are an enemy of tramps everywhere. I noticed though, when he opened his book, that when Milou barked the speech-bubble read 'Waouf, waouf', whereas all our dogs in Britain make a more manly 'Woof, woof'. How can we possibly have a truly Common Market when such fundamental divisions exist, I asked myself ('Je me demande' as the French would say. An excellent name for a gangster I have always thought: Jimmy Demand).

The *clochard* left, as he saw a couple of policemen coming, carefully hiding the bit of cardboard he had been sleeping on behind a buttress, and told me he would be back later.

I went back to the barge and as I did so the police arrived and asked me whether the *clochard* had been bothering me and then, like all policemen, started to ask me what I was doing and whether I had permission to be here at all. I have always believed that if you reply with sufficient authority more often than not the police will give up, and in this case they clearly felt that they were out of their depth and that if there was a problem it was definitely the responsibility of some other department.

I locked up and went to see a musician friend of mine, who lived in the Marais, a district of Paris that had once been marsh ground. Paris has the best urban transportation system of any great city that I know, the métro and the buses run regularly and they go very close to your destination. In years of making big-budget films, I had always taken taxis in Paris, but it was Michel who explained the subtleties of the system. As a leading expert on medieval music, he is constantly travelling round Paris and the world with his three-man group, and has a vast experience of waiting at airports for cultural attachés who do not turn up. He has therefore developed a knowledge of speedy urban transport systems which is second to none, and has convincingly proved to me that the transport provided by the city of Paris is quicker than taxis.

To arrive at your destination in Paris is one thing but unless you have the mind of a mathematical genius, it is vital to have written down the door codes that all Parisian houses seem to have these days. Most large houses which have been split up into flats have concierges (who are almost entirely Portuguese), which means that during the day the gates to the courtyards are open, but at night or at the weekends the only way to get in is to have the door code, as none of the entry systems have talk buttons. I had forgotten the code, of course, and had to wait like a cat until someone came back from their shopping, and slip in with them. Like many old houses in Paris, it has a superb staircase made from oak and marble – the kind of construction that has stood the test of time for four centuries, but would not be passed by any local district surveyor in Britain today on the grounds that it would be unsafe in case of fire.

A delicious meal of broccoli and spaghetti was waiting, cooked by my friend's wife, a talented designer from Marseilles. The French have a talent, I believe, for being able to cook almost anything and make it taste delicious. They are, surprisingly, extremely precise in the way they prepare their food. All this domestic knowledge was suddenly becoming very important to me, for before I started on this voyage I had always had someone to look after me. While I had cooked the occasional meal I had never had to look after a household on a day-to-day basis, or to wash my clothes. Even when I had first moved to London and lived in a chummery in Pont Street, there had been someone to mastermind the household shopping. Before the days of launderettes, the laundry was delivered once a week in hard cardboard containers which were swapped for similar ones stuffed full of dirty washing. Heaven help you if you missed a week. Middle age is not usually the time to start being concerned about such things, but life on board in a confined space was very much conditioned by mess and planning.

In the second week in June, everyone who can play a note of music and quite a few who cannot, practise in the streets for the recently inaugurated 'night of music', which the city fathers have decided should fall on the shortest night of the year, the summer solstice, 21 June. As I walked back to the boat I passed every possible type of musician, from a fine chamber group playing Mozart in the Place des Vosges, to a young English trombonist with his jazz band, tearing it off on the Île St Louis bridge with an excellent rendition of 'After You've Gone'.

My musician friend and I called in to a pastry shop called Charlotte de Ville and talk to the proprietress who was known for her eccentric chocolate cakes and her poems. We sat in a darkened room at the back of the shop as an out-of-work Argentinian actress recited some of the boss's poetry, while she sat purring behind a large chocolate shoe with the Little Prince's flower, also in chocolate, stuck into it on a stick. Here was a side of Paris that put me well out of my depth. This huge lady with her sweet smile and cottage-loaf bun, looking just like a culinary Madame Arcati, the clairvoyant from *Blithe Spirit*, and her friend – who was clearly an accomplished actress – must have had some secret which was completely lost on me. Perhaps my French is not what it should be.

I left the cake shop alone and wandered back to the Pont des Arts, picking my way through the lovers and dogs. In Paris you must, apparently, have a lover or a dog. Walking either seems to follow approximately the same routine. The canine card-leaving occurs with approximately the same frequency as the osculatory pause. I need not have felt lonely, for when I reached the *Leo* she had become the centre of attention for a group of strollers. In no time at all I was answering all types of questions on our route so far, and where we were going. Most of the questioners found it hard to believe that we had crossed the Channel in such an unusual craft, but all said they would like to come along. I suppose the water is extremely romantic on a hot summer's afternoon in a big city.

A good-looking American girl-jogger brazenly asked if she could have a drink of water. I foolishly obliged. Within minutes she had uncoiled into the most ferocious bore – just like one of those Chinese flowers made of paper that expand when put in water. Why could she not come with us? Did I dislike women? 'No, no, no,' I almost screamed. I began to have a sinking feeling that I was not going to get rid of her unless I moved very fast. She had that terrible attitude which many foreigners have in France, that if you speak English then you must be their friend. Desperately I thought of what a Frenchman would do in such circumstances but the possibilities required a kind of *sang-froid* I could not muster. Thankfully I remembered that the owner of the beautiful old Dutch barge, the *Souqui*, which was moored a few metres up-stream, had told me to visit him any evening. I made a firm but final excuse, and almost pushing my visitor off the barge, locked up. It had been a lesson in how very careful one has to be about the occasional groupie: if she had stayed there a moment longer, I am quite sure that she would never have left.

The difference between the little *Leo* and the other barges moored along the Left Bank was that the *Leo* was clearly a travelling barge rather than a sedate houseboat. The *Souqui* was the doyenne of the houseboat fleet. Built in 1890 in Holland, she had been beautifully repaired, and converted to the floating equivalent of an expensive house in Chelsea. She had been a sailing barge, and, according to her owner, an energetic art director from the movie world, had taken cargoes as far as Ceylon, though I suspect he had been reading too much Conrad. She had all her masts and deck furniture, and huge leeboards, and all were painted and varnished. Below decks had been furnished like a London club, with many leather armchairs and solid furniture.

My host was struggling with the Achilles-heel of all boats, his lavatory. His son's girlfriend had deposited some unmentionable in it and it had become blocked. I think the poor girl had been unfairly blamed, for in my opinion if there is a woman about when something goes wrong on board, she will automatically get the blame. In my more fanciful moments, I have wondered whether the jealous feminine spirit of a boat somehow plays tricks on certain female visitors in this way, because some do seem to me to be abnormally accident-prone. I attempted to help to clear the blockage by lending my dinghy and rowing it round to the side of the barge, so that the offending mass could be poked at from the outside. As it turned out, time and caustic soda would, it seemed, be the only solution for clearing the problem, so I found myself yarning with this putative mariner. He was full of plans for sailing away and doing what I was doing, but his problem was that he had just about the best mooring in any city in the world at No. 1 Paris. The most elegant of all Paris's magnificent bridges, the Pont Neuf, lay a hundred metres upstream, he had water and electricity permanently plumbed in, telephones were everywhere. Even when he has made all the sails, I do not think that the *Souqui* will ever pass downstream under the Pont des Arts.

The *Leo* had been in Paris now for nearly a week. Ray had returned and we were getting the urge to move our mooring. It is an affliction that I suppose all travellers suffer from, especially when all that is required for a change of view is to move one's home, as it were, round the corner. We decided to see what the canals that pierce the heart of Paris were like, returning to the Pont des Arts in time for the night of music which, if the towpath practising was anything to go by, was going to be a noisy affair. We left early on a beautiful summer's morning with a thick mist on the river which obligingly cleared enough for us to see the magnificent spires of Notre Dame silhouetted against a bright blue sky, as though perched on a bed of snowy white clouds. A child's view of heaven, perhaps, but one that would do very well.

Our first stop was to be the *'village du vin'* near the Pont de Bercy. I had first been introduced to this sprawling Napoleonic compound, that stretches over many acres, in the 1960s, when I used to help a friend who was very conscious of the price of everything to bring a barrel of claret back to London. I soon found this procedure was more romantic than practical: the complication of corking the bottles once the wine had been decanted was simply not worth the effort. I decided it was better to drink less wine and buy a bottle when required. This time I decided I would buy a small barrel and draw off what we needed after a suitable period of time.

We moored and walked to the wine village which is still remarkably unspoiled, but alas, as is so often the case with places that have retained a little charm and not been mauled by the developers, the place was being used as a film location. German soldiers of the Third Reich were everywhere, marching bands of presumably Free French through swirling clouds of man-made fog. The telltale signs of a film crew were everywhere. Polystyrene cups littered the moss-covered pavements, the gutters were lined with cables from a generator, groups of those special winsome children that are always used in films were being frightfully good, the caterers were already laying out the tables for lunch in an empty wine shed. I am afraid that film crews are a bit like the ravens in *Zuleika Dobson*, whose arrival is a portent of imminent disaster – in this case the developers who will surely smash this charming place and build some useless sports palace where performance drugs will replace nectar from Bordeaux.

Ray and I did a great deal of tasting, spitting out the samples in the required manner. We decided on a Bordeaux which would have had a fancy label stuck on it in London and would have been sold for ten times the price we were paying – but we had forgotten the barrel itself which brought the price up substantially. Pleasantly reinforced by what we had imbibed, we set about trying to get our heavy barrel back to the *Leo*. I wished I had unloaded the car, but in the end we persuaded the gentleman who had filled our barrel to run us back in his van. He was rewarded with a pack of duty-free cigarettes, which I had great difficulty in making him accept.

Getting the heavy barrel on to the boat was a job for the crane I had built. Without any design, its construction had

been very much a question of trial and error. I had managed
to get it to lift our little 2CV on and off, but it was a performance not lightly entered into. Ray, however, was able to
demonstrate the barrel hitch, a knot rarely used in these
days, and we had the barrel on board just in time, as a dock
inspector came along and told us that loading merchandise
required a licence. I am afraid that we both pretended that
we did not understand French and he finally gave up with a
good deal of *sotto voce* cursing. I could not feel guilty about
this minuscule infringement of the rules.

We left to go downstream to the entrance of the Canal St
Martin, where we had to wait until the traffic lights turned
in our favour. The traffic is one way for twenty minutes every
hour, a rule that is very strictly controlled by the river police,
whose headquarters are just upstream of the Île St Louis.
The barges, of course, know these rules, and if for some
reasons the lights are held because some huge pusher barge
is working its way upstream, they are able to time their arrival
so they can go straight downstream as the lights change. I
was not aware how difficult it would be to stop because of
the current under us, and so we took a turn on a steel ring
in a buttress under one of the bridges, to wait for the lights
to change. Within seconds we were spotted by the river
police. They leapt into an inflatable dinghy with an Alsatian
in its bows, and roared up to us. We all growled at each
other and before pencils could be licked we had let go and
slipped into the lock at the Bassin d'Arsenal, which has
been turned from a sand and gravel dock to a very smart
marina full of expensive plastic boats. This was no place
for the battered old *Leo*, and in any case there was no space
for us. We made our way up through the marina, very much
aware of what it feels like to be looked down the nose
upon.

In front of us lay a tunnel that passes under the column
marking the storming of the Bastille. There were only seven
prisoners there at the time, which must have been a great

disappointment for the mob: six political prisoners and one old man of eighty, the reason for whose imprisonment no one, apparently, could remember. The interior of the tunnel is a magnificent sight. We went through in the early afternoon, when the cavernous darkness was lit by great slanting shafts of sunlight from ventilation holes in the Boulevard Richard Lenoir above. The canal had been covered in the nineteenth century in an attempt to ease the road-traffic problem: how optimistic mankind can be! In the days we were in Paris, the tabloid press had been full of lurid stories of how a band of cannibals had been discovered living in the darkness of the tunnel, but there was no evidence of any life at all with the exception of a few rats on the tow-path. The paths at either end have been blocked off to stop people walking through on their own, probably a very sensible precaution as otherwise it would become a muggers' paradise.

At the other end of the tunnel the canal opens into the heart of Paris, which forms a great contrast to the Seine. Tall buildings with shops and cafés are only a street's width away from the canal. I stopped besides the Hôtel du Nord which Arletty had frequented in the film of that name. The building is uninhabited and derelict now, but the government, to their credit, have decided to call it a national monument, and so it will be preserved.

Paris has always been a sanctuary for talented foreigners: exiles from repression of some sort, or people from other countries who have simply fallen in love with the city. I left Ray with the boat and went to see one of the most astonishing men that I have ever met: Rostislav Doboujinsky, an émigré Russian designer with whom I had worked long ago and who was my youngest daughter's godfather.

His studio lay not far from the canal up a dirty staircase in a rundown block of workshops catering for every type of trade, from printers to metal workers. Inside the door, in fact as you step through almost any front door in Paris, the world changes entirely: suddenly I found myself in theatrical Paris. 'Tonton', as everybody calls him, has spent his eighty-seven years never specializing in anything but having experience of just about everything. His father had been a designer for Diaghilev, and he himself had been brought up in pre-revolutionary St Petersburg, only leaving Russia in 1925, by which time he had travelled extensively with his father – all over Europe and the States. His intimate knowledge of wild-life had made it possible for him to make the brilliant masks for the film I made with my wife, *The Tales of Beatrix Potter*. He was currently making vast chandeliers for some magnate in Madrid.

I wanted to refresh my memory about edible fungi, about which, naturally, he knew a great deal, and in a very Russian way: he knew exactly which mushrooms were poisonous, and not those which were edible. This roundabout way of approaching a potentially dangerous problem was simple and easy, and revealed to me a kind of lateral thinking that has been extremely useful in my travels. Being a consummate artist, he drew me some clear sketches of the types we might encounter in Burgundy and further east on the banks of the Danube. He had learnt a lot about mushrooms when he was in the Russian boy scouts during the early days of the Revolution. Food was extremely scarce in St Petersburg and he and his troop had gone out into the woods to scour them for mushrooms. Whenever I have been hunting mushrooms with him, I have watched him bite off a very small bit of a possibly suspect one, then spit it out immediately. He says that all the ones that are not obviously poisonous, but doubtful, taste very peppery and should not be eaten. He also has a marvellous system for pickling mushrooms in vinegar, a little sugary syrup and herbs, thus preserving them in jars for many months.

Our mooring near the Bassin de Villettes was quite peaceful and so far we had had no problems with *'voyous'*, the lay-abouts that we were always being warned about by the well-to-do. So, throwing caution to the winds, Ray and I set out for the Balajo, which lies in the Rue de la Harpe, a little street at the back of the Place de la Bastille. The Balajo is an old-time dance hall which still has a *'bal musette'*, the French equivalent to a tea dance, on Monday afternoons and Friday evenings. The significance of this particular timetable was not clear to us until later. In the eternal search for the real Mimi and Fifi, a non-tourist place like the Balajo seemed a good place to look, or so I thought. It was Friday evening and when we arrived the *bal* was in full swing. The entrance was well endowed with bouncers who told me firmly that I had to leave my camera in the cloakroom. The camera would not have worked inside, in any case, as it was almost pitch dark, but as our eyes grew accustomed to the level of light I was able to make out an extravagant, late-forties decor, with lots of leaning lamp-posts and tiny bulbs glinting through holes in painted plywood. The floor was packed with couples, while the band on the podium smashed out a spirited version of the 'Sheikh of Araby'.

After a few minutes, I plucked up enough courage to ask a neighbour why the management was so strict about photography. He shrugged his shoulders as though it was a childish question and explained that on Friday nights and Monday afternoons most of the small shopkeepers and businessmen had time off, and this was where they all came for an illicit fling, presumably with their Mimis and Fifis; or, in the case of the ladies, to dance with some of the professional gigolos who were sitting at the tables round us. There was a tremendous sense of cool, of people knowing just what was what. If the ladies wanted to dance with a particular man, the smallest smile or nod would be sufficient for the gentleman to cross the floor and ask the woman to dance. Most of these men would dance with the palm of the hand that would normally be pressed on the woman's back folded outwards. Intimacy came later perhaps. There were hardly any smiles, but there was clearly a good deal of pleasure being had in a subdued sort of way. Fearful of putting my foot in it and perhaps being knifed by some furious *charcutier* because I had asked his *vendeuse* from a boutique near the Gare de Lyon to take a turn on the floor, and also because it was clear that our Mimi and Fifi were not here, Ray and I left, whistling a nostalgic tune or two from the Piaf selection that the band had been playing.

The next day, we moved on a little through the Bassin de Villettes, through the locations where *Les Enfants du Paradis* was shot in the last days of the war, under constant harassment from the Nazis. I stopped at the nearest point to the Gare du Nord to visit another expatriate, Anthony Sidey, an Englishman who has been living in Paris for twenty-five years doing what he first dreamt of doing when he was eleven: making and playing harpsichords. His workshop, in a cul-de-sac overlooking the rail marshalling yard outside the Gare du Nord, was a jumble of bent and drying wood, mixed with old musical instruments that had been sent there for repair or that he had bought for restoration. When I arrived, Anthony was sitting at a beautiful harpsichord that he had built, practising for his own pleasure. It takes him seven years to build a harpsichord from the moment that he cuts the first bit of wood and shapes it the way he wants. When the instruments are finished they are quite magnificent, and Anthony, a Francophile *par excellence*, prefers not to export them but rather to keep them in France for visiting virtuosi to play on their tours. I think he does not really like to see these beautiful things go too far away. It is unusual for such a talented musician to be able to build such highly prized instruments.

It was time now to end our perambulation round Paris and return to the Pont des Arts for the night of music, and rendezvous with my daughter Daisy and her husband Marcus. Luckily our mooring under the bridge was still free, but

113

we only just pipped a hotel barge to the post. There was a certain amount of argument but in the end he agreed to drop back and tie up against one of the barges a little further down river. To celebrate the night of music and my daughter's arrival, I had decided to have a dinner party on the deck of the barge and invite some friends. Bruno, a director of photography with more feel for the medium than most of his calling, was an excellent cook and prepared a very simple meal from leeks and a shin of veal. As it turned out, his reputation as a chef was guaranteed to remain safe, even had the meal not been delicious: no sooner had the musical celebrations started than all traffic came to a standstill, preventing the guests, with the exception of Daisy and Marcus, arriving. Moreover, our berth had become untenable because a really loud and astonishingly bad rock band had come to play no more than ten feet from the barge. While some of the smaller bands on the bridge above us were attracting large groups to hear them play, the band next to us seemed to have found the secret of actually repelling an audience. While all types of illegal substances were clearly being passed around, there was no sign of any reduction in the dreary decibels that were pumping from the vibrating but obviously robust loudspeakers. Ray and I decided to cast off and move up the river to tie up on the *quai* just below Notre Dame, which I am sure was illegal, but a crimette that we hoped would go unnoticed on a night such as this.

As we sat down to eat, the heavens opened for a few minutes and we all crouched under our blue awning holding our plates. Suddenly there was a piercing scream from Daisy who had been standing beneath part of the awning that had, we later discovered, been weakened by a burning cigarette butt thrown from the bridge above us at the Pont des Arts. The sudden shower had formed a large puddle in the canvas and the pressure had produced a fine jet of water which had gone down Daisy's neck. Her scream passed practically unnoticed in the cacophony all around us. Bands were marching over the Pont Neuf; African groups were celebrating Sainte Cecilia's night with the wildest heathen music; on the opposite bank a lone violinist was making a poor attempt at a spirited Hungarian melody; and a beautiful blonde flautist was playing under the plane tree to which we had moored the barge.

The night was clear and fresh now, after the rain, and this vast tempest of sound was being echoed from one disapproving building to another, bouncing away down the river, never quite dying away before it was replaced by another squall of sound. The new tablecloth that I had bought for the occasion was soaked and the plates that we had laid for the absent guests had puddles of water in them. We dried the seats, opened a bottle or two of the cheap champagne we had bought near Rheims, and settled down to watch the spectacle and to wave at the *bateaux mouches*, those enormous glass structures that glide past by the minute, their loudspeakers blasting out essential tourist facts in every language known to man.

Much later we returned to our mooring under the Pont des Arts. The noisy band was still just as noisy but the gaps between numbers had increased substantially. The possibility of sleep was remote, so Daisy and I decided to take a walk round the crowded streets. In the Rue de Seine a raucous band dressed entirely in red plastic, too tight for comfort or decorum, was playing to a crowd of dancing students. The lead trumpeter was disturbing the rhythm with his attempts to tantalize the crowd by pulling down the bottom part of his plastic outfit and giving them a glimpse of pubic hair. The crowd were distinctly untantalized and the lady tuba player, wearing dark glasses and a trilby, stepped forward and briskly pulled his trousers down, so indicating in a perfectly French fashion that there was nothing there to make a fuss about. The music improved and Daisy and I joined the dancers on that warm summer's night. I was filled with admiration that French law has it that every month for one night, everyone is allowed to make as much noise as he likes. Bravo, Paris.

CHAPTER SEVEN
Paris to Montbard

One day we just had to leave Paris: the itch to start the motor and get on our way again, never knowing where we would stop for the night, was irresistible. We pulled away from the Pont des Arts in the dawn with the guardian *clochard* fast asleep in a huddled bundle on his favourite piece of cardboard. The morning light was slanting across the *quais* and the noise of the traffic was reduced to the sound of a single vehicle. The air was cool and fresh as we passed under the shadow of Notre Dame for the last time, and made our way up the Seine under the Pont de Bercy.

Just past the bridge, we passed a barge called the *Sylphe* which had been there when we loaded our barrel of wine on board. Her captain, a grumpy chap with a saint for a wife, told me he had to feed his family on the equivalent of four hundred pounds a month and, with five mouths to feed, found this very hard. I waved as we went past and he told me that he would be following us in a few days because he had got a cargo of barley to transport to Basel in Switzerland. A drought in the USA had caused panic in the grain futures market, and for some reason large amounts of wheat and barley were being moved from the huge Common Market silos to Switzerland. From time to time the mysteries of commerce elude me, but this *batelier* was a good deal happier than when I had last encountered him. Every cloud has a silver lining for someone somewhere, they say.

It took us longer to push up against the current than I'd anticipated, and it was early afternoon before we reached the junction of the Marne and the Seine. I then took the kind of decision that you can only take when you do not have hotels booked or appointments to keep: I decided to divert from our planned route, and turned left, or, more nautically, to port, up the Marne. I had always wanted to visit Joinville, famous for its film studios, and had once passed that way on one of my earlier voyages, but been unable to stop. It was not very far out of our way and we reached the suburb of Paris in time to moor early.

Joinville still has villas from the 1900s stretched along the banks of the Marne, which gives it a sleepy, long-ago feeling – of dusty roads rather than streets and shady plane trees. We tied up outside a jolly-looking restaurant where a huge, cutout plywood chef, dominating the skyline, announced that this was Chez Gegène. The whole scene could have been lifted from the pages of *Babar the Elephant*: even the scullers seemed to have slowed down to the pace of the summer's evening, dipping the blades of their oars languorously into the glassy surface of the water with a satisfying swish.

Ray and I smartened ourselves up and went into the huge restaurant which was also a *bal musette*. There were half a dozen couples dancing to a live band. Inside the building and outside under umbrellas, people were eating and laughing. The menu, as in all good restaurants in France or anywhere else, was extremely simple: either lobster or steak and chips. The kitchen, which was outside, was manned by twenty swift and swearing waiters using the shortest slang abbreviations for their orders. The final dressings on the plates were dished out by the owner's extremely pretty daughter. Ray and I ate our meal and reminisced about the trip so far while watching the dancers. There was a woman of fifty summers, who looked exactly like Toulouse Lautrec's favourite dancer, La Goulue, dancing with a short fat man of the same age. His shirt, open to the waist, revealed a huge and hairy expanse of flesh. They made an odd couple, but they danced beautifully to an accordion version of a song

118

called 'Au près de ma blonde', and one by one the other dancers sat down to let these two have the floor.

Somehow, the music and the setting made me feel extremely apprehensive about the journey I had planned. Would we ever find anywhere as accessible as France? Although Ray's French was improving enough to be able to order his own meal, we both decided that now we were under way again, we would give up restaurants and live off our own cooking. We walked the few yards back to the boat and I pointed out the Joinville film studios to him. It is a mystery to me why film studios have to look so ugly from the outside. I suppose they are no more so than any factory, but somehow it seems odd that such varied and extravagant products should emerge from these utilitarian buildings.

The next morning we turned the *Leo* around and went down the Marne till we reached the Seine. Turning upstream we passed through the stockbroker belt, where trim expensive houses and trim expansive lawns stretched down to the river, its banks lined with weeping willows. There were many gorgeous females busy browning themselves for God knows what, but though we went very close and did our most charming waves, we never got so much as a flicker of recognition in return. Suddenly all my warm feelings for the French, from the night before at Chez Gegène, evaporated. Here were rich, superior beings who clearly believed that the sun was there to shine only on their posteriors, and that the very idea of a battered old boat like ours approaching within waving distance was too much. The rich are different, and their attitude prompted some wry and rudely accurate remarks from Ray, normally charitable about his fellow beings.

The beautiful wooded banks through Fontainebleau led us to our mooring, in the mouth of a stream near Montereau. Ray got out his fishing line and tried his luck, while I started to read a story called 'The Two Hundred Pound Millionaire'. From a collection by Weston Martyr called *The Pipe Pushers*, it is a tale of courage and self-reliance which I highly rec-

119

ommend to any voyager, and also to anyone who tries to judge people by their appearance. It reminded me of an occasion when I was growing up in India: my father heard me complaining about the five-day journey that we were making from Bombay to the Himalayas, and insisted that I read *The Worst Journey in the World* by Apsley Cherry-Garrard – the story of a disastrous expedition to the Antarctic, organized to collect the eggs of the emperor penguin. He was right to think that, having read that book, no one had the right to complain about discomfort while travelling.

The morning trip to the *boulangerie* took us through narrow streets to the usual comforting French square, its patch of sandy gravel dented by the impact of a myriad steel *boules*, thrown with accuracy and venom. *Boules*, or *pétanque* as it is known in the South, is the only game I know that rivals the subterfuge and meanness of croquet. I had, by now, fallen into the French habit of buying bread every day. French bread never seems to keep for more than a few hours, and croissants are at their best when still hot, the fat in which they have been cooked staining the sides of the plain white paper bags they all seem to come in.

As Ray and I strolled back from the village, we discussed the latest problem we were having with the steering of the boat. I felt that the fins that we had welded on to the rudder in London, and that had subsequently vibrated off, would have been a great help with the steering in the narrow rivers where we were having difficulty in turning. I had heard that there was a boatyard owned by a certain Mr Evans, who had to be English, in Sens – a town an hour or two away – and I thought that before we went into the wilds of the Canal de Bourgogne we ought to have the fins put on again.

Mr Evans was indeed English and from the British Navy. He had tried to set up his business on the Thames, but his speciality, namely repairing wooden boats, was considered too messy for the riparian authorities in the Home Counties, so he had tossed his curls, so to speak, ventured into the

Common Market, found things much easier to manage, and really felt, he said, that he had the right to exist here. As luck would have it, he had ordered a mobile crane that day, to lift some boats that had been stored in his yard back into the water; so we soon had the *Leo* on the bank for a welding job on the rudder. Though we had all the apparatus for welding neither of us had enough skill, so we recruited a friendly Dutchman who was building a hotel barge nearby and had run out of money. He was an extremely good welder and had our job done in a very short space of time. In the half an hour or so that the boat was out of the water, he managed somehow not only to tell us his entire life story, but also to ring up the local newspaper and tell them that we, an English boat, had stopped here for him to make repairs. Two reporters arrived and interviewed the Dutchman, who seemed to be a natural for that sort of thing, about his life and hard times – and they took a picture of the *Leo*.

We gave the voluble Dutchman a lift back to his barge while he explained what his perfect woman would be like. She would have to be a non-smoking vegetarian with a degree in handling repairs to boat engines, and would only speak when spoken to. I could see, as he prattled away, that he was unlikely to find his ideal mate. His parting salvo, as he left us in one of the quaint, sloping-sided locks that they have on the upper reaches of the Seine, was about how to tie up. His advice, when we tried it in the next lock, was quite useless, but he did know how to weld – which is by no means as simple as it looks. My first job ever had been in a factory in Wolverhampton, spot-welding steel folding chairs. I think I must have ruined the production figures for the weeks I was there before being fired, because I never developed the necessary lightness of touch to stop the welding flame burning through the metal in the wrong places.

The sloping-sided locks were difficult for us, because we were not quite long enough to stretch from one end to the other as a normal barge would do, which prevented us from

121

making fast on the upright portions at the ends of the lock. They were far from being a source of grief to all, however. The one we encountered after leaving the Dutchman provided recreation for a family of ducklings, who were having the greatest time skiing down the slippery, sloping sides of the lock. The mother stood watchfully on the top of the lock making sure all was well, and the goody-goody of the family stood next to her. I am always astonished by how much young humans resemble young things of all other species. As the lock filled, the ducklings rejoined their mother to wait for another vessel to go through, and more sliding fun.

The Dutchman's work on the rudder had improved the steering and he had made all sorts of rash promises about what he would do if the fins fell off, though, as he had used much heavier steel plate to make the fins and had double welded the joints, it was, in his view, quite impossible that this should happen. Only time would tell.

Towards evening we met some Swiss damsels in distress. A brother and sister and the boy's girlfriend had hired a holiday boat and had run out of diesel. Running out of diesel in a boat is bad news because in my experience it always leads to other troubles that you have not anticipated. We gave them some of our fuel, but the motor refused to start even with Ray's nimble fingers stripping the filters far into the night. They were in some distress as they were far from any telephone and did not know what to do. We told them we would give them a tow in the morning, to somewhere they could ring the hire company and get their boat fixed.

The young man turned out to be a trainee chef, and the girls were training to be teachers of handicrafts. They offered to cook us a Swiss lunch the following day, while they waited for their boat to be repaired. As I lay in bed that night I remembered David Lean telling me how he had been walking round Shah Jahan's gardens in the Red Fort at Delhi, with a famous bestseller writer who had been sent out to work with him on a script about the Taj Mahal. The distinguished writer had fallen madly in love with a Swiss girl in the hotel where he was staying, and as he walked round the gardens he was heard to mutter, 'If there be paradise on earth, it is Swiss, it is Swiss, it is Swiss.'

Our Swiss girls, pretty and practical, leapt ashore when we reached the nearest town and went shopping for a memorable feast, in which there were a great many potatoes and raw carrots. A grumpy Yorkshireman came to mend their boat and complained that the boat-hire companies were a scandal: they never spent enough money maintaining their fleets and the boats were forever breaking down and spoiling holidays. It occurred to me that this dyspeptic monologue could well have been a defence mechanism and that he was probably one of the owners himself. He soon had the engine running again, however, and the Swiss went on their way.

Soon after setting off up the green and lush valley of the Seine, we encountered a dredger barge, which we accompanied through a number of locks. The family who ran it were the third generation of *bateliers* to work on this stretch of the river, preventing it from silting up. They were hired on a contract basis, being directed to whatever part of the river the authorities thought it necessary to dredge. I was impressed by the clever idea for stabilizing the barge which they had developed. The barge had a dredger grab on it, and when the grab lifted its bucket from the bottom of the river with upwards of five tons of silt in it, the barge would, without a stabilizer, naturally start to list – which could be dangerous, and very annoying for mum in the kitchen. To compensate, they had made some enormous legs out of steel pipes. These they lowered through holes in the bottom of the barge with their crane, and then fixed them so that they held the vessel steady.

They told me that they were kept busy all year round dredging away, even though the barge traffic was declining year by year. It would be a bad day if the powers that be stopped keeping the upper part of the Seine open for river traffic, although it must be extremely expensive and increasingly hard to justify.

At Cézy lock there was a letter waiting for me from my son Jason, who was in China researching a book he was writing on tea. I am always immensely impressed by postal services that can cope with mail for itinerants. The 'poste restante' system works extremely well in France providing that you remember to take your passport when you go to collect your mail. Of course when you have a boat the mail is given to the boat rather than an individual, but it is very important that the sender addresses the letter to a lock in a town and not some sleepy corner where the lock-keeper could easily forget to give it to you. My letter was handed to me by a very jolly man who greeted the boat with, 'Ah, ma petite *Leontyne*', as though a long-lost lover had walked up his garden path. He turned the letter over and over in his hand before giving it to me, as though he was reluctant to part with it, and then told me that as there were no barges coming I could stay in the lock till I had read it. He was clearly very curious to know what was in this mysterious missive from the East. I told him that it was from my son and that he had written to say that he would be meeting us in Montbard, where I had said we would be for the celebrations on 14 July, Bastille Day. He seemed enormously gratified that someone so very far away from France had been thinking about the fall of the Bastille and the abolition of the monarchy.

It had rained a good deal that day and since there was a thunderstorm on its way, I decided to moor near some tourist boats, something that I try to avoid whenever possible. The barge and the tug together weigh about sixty tons and to make a firm mooring it is necessary to find a tree if there are no bollards about. In this case the trees were on the other side of the towpath – a problem, as it is completely forbidden to stretch ropes across the paths, as they are always being used by the lock-keepers and their families riding *mobylettes* – the motorized bicycles that everyone seems to own in the

124

countryside in France. Many are the accidents that have been caused by mooring ropes catching the wheels of the bicycles and pitching the riders over the handlebars. I had had some long steel pegs made before leaving England for such emergencies and I used them now, although it was difficult to get a firm fixing in the crumbling bank of the Canal de Bourgogne and I had to use our fourteen-pound sledgehammer to drive the pegs into the side of the path. The noise of the hammer striking the steel pegs aroused a party of Germans on the tourist boat near us, and suddenly, as I bent over my work, I found myself staring into the malevolent face of a huge Alsatian dog. The beefy owner announced that he and his wife had locked up the children and were taking the dog for a walk, which seemed an orderly if somewhat inhuman way of going about things. I wondered what it is like to take one's pets on holiday, something that I suppose very few Britons can remember doing nowadays.

The threatened thunderstorm arrived in style. We battened down the hatch, and as we listened to the rain pounding on the steel deck of the barge, Ray told me that lightning jumps upwards from the earth, rather than the other way about as I had imagined. It was not till the morning that we realized that in our haste we had left the cable that linked the barge and the tug on the deck, where the plug had dropped into a pool of water. This had caused a short and the batteries on the tug had gone completely flat. I am always extremely apprehensive about electrical supplies on boats and though I thought I had taken every precaution, it proved to be a problem to start the *Leo*'s engine. I had a 12-kilowatt generator on the barge but I did not have a suitable charger for the 24-volt batteries on the *Leo*. The batteries on the barge were charged with a trickle charger from the generator and from the engine on the tug when it was running. After trying to bring the tug alongside the barge to jump-start it, only to discover that the cables were not heavy enough and melting them – then having to pull the *Leo* out of the way of an angry, oncoming barge that did not have the room to pass – we were exhausted. I decided that, cost what it may, I would take the bicycle and buy some flexible welding cable from the nearby town of St Florentin. I find that the French have an extremely good distribution of professional equipment, and was pleased to find a shop almost immediately that could sell me what I required. The ten metres of half-inch-diameter flexible copper wire cost me over a hundred pounds. This was not what I was expecting but at least I now have the consolation of being the proud possessor of what are probably the most expensive jump leads in the world.

During my chat with the shopkeeper he told me that they made an excellent cheese in this little town and that there was a cheese works at the back of his shop. De Gaulle once said in despair that it was hard to govern a country with so many different types of cheese, each with its own band of fervent supporters. The cheese they make in St Florentin is soft, white, bland, and has the consistency of foam rubber. Why it should be so sought after baffles me. Touching it reminded me of being acutely embarrassed as a young assistant director on a Western film in Spain, when the star, Jayne Mansfield, invited me to feel her magnificent bosom for the silicone implant that had recently been injected by the studio doctors. Her husband, Johnny Haggerty, was Mr Universe and was extremely proud of his wife's figure: they were busily merchandising their superb physiques with the Johnny and Jayne bodybuilding kit. Despite this memory, I was forced to buy some of the cheese which, to my astonishment, Ray devoured with apparent enjoyment.

With the right equipment, the Gardner engine started at once and we were on our way again, through countryside that was beginning to look like the tourist posters for France that you see on the underground. There were a large number of locks on this stretch of canal, manned by a variety of people, mostly women. At one flight of locks where there were two locks separated by two hundred yards of canal, I came across an ancient feud. The woman at the lower lock spent the whole time we were with her bitching about the woman at the next lock. She was obviously more engrossed in complaining about her neighbour than attending to her garden or house, which was a mess. When we got to the upper lock of this pair, the lock lady was trim, with dyed hair and a garden as neat as a pin. When I complimented her on the care she had taken of her domain, she said, with what I thought was a twinkle in her eye, that she had a lot of help from the chap who lived at the lock we had just come through. There was clearly a good deal going on on this little *bief* that I would never know.

The Swiss boat we had towed had passed us when we broke down, and now we passed them as they were handing their boat back to the hire company where it had come from. We stopped to say goodbye again, and to fill up our water tank. As we did so, we chatted with the man in charge who had pulled up in his little van and left the engine running. After a few minutes, when we had agreed to pay for the water, the hooter in his van started to blow. I looked up to see a large Labrador at the wheel who was pushing the hooter button with its paw: something that it had apparently learnt to do itself when it thought its master had spent long enough on his business. A neat trick, but not one that I would care to teach a dog.

That night I made a really stupid mistake which reminded me of a comment that Patrick Leigh Fermor wrote, about an extremely well-known and expensive London restaurant, in the suggestion book at the Travellers' Club. He simply wrote the name of the restaurant and beside it, in the comments column, drew a skull and crossbones. I had purchased the Michelin Guide and noticed that, in Tonnerre, there was one of those grand restaurants with a top rating. Ray and I walked up the hill to the old abbey where the restaurant was, and as soon as I was inside I realized what a mistake I had made. The place was full of the kind of motorist who has taken the

Hovercraft over the Channel, avoided the traffic in Paris, averaged so many miles per hour and so on, facts which they bray at each other over their quails' eggs. It took us three hours to get some soup and chops. I think we would both have walked out before finishing the overrated, overpriced offerings served on vast plates, had it not been pouring with rain outside, and a long walk home to the *Leo*.

From Tonnerre we went through one of the most beautiful parts of the Canal de Bourgogne, which many are trying to turn into a national monument, whilst others wish to reduce the running costs by installing automatic locks to do the work of the very varied selection of lock-keepers who currently look after them. One of the lady lock-minders was an out-of-work hairdresser whose salon, in the neighbouring town, had been closed down. I badly needed a haircut and had some scissors with me, so I asked whether she would oblige, and she did a very nice job whilst waiting for the next boat to come through. She told me that she had a free house with the job, that there was not very much to do, and that life was quite agreeable, although she had not yet experienced a winter there. A few locks further on we bought some really excellent wine from a woman who clearly caught the bottles as they fell off the back of a lorry. We stopped at Lock 72, having passed through thirty locks that day – and had a haircut! Not bad for one day. The exercise had purged the disgust I felt with myself for having gone to the expensive clip joint the night before. The pirate flag should have flown from those towers, but then I suppose they give their customers what they want: isolation from reality and a car park.

The toothless lock-lady at number 72 had sold me some lemons and I cooked spaghetti with lemon and cream sauce which was a good deal more agreeable than our last evening meal. The locks shut at 7.30 p.m. in those parts, so apart from tidying the boat up and checking the engine, cooking, fishing and reading were our evening activities. Ray's attempts to catch fish were not very successful, but he was practising for the Bastille Day fishing competition that we had seen advertised for Montbard, where I hoped we would be to meet Jason.

It was a full day's journey to Montbard and we had two days to get there before all the locks closed for the holiday, so I decided to visit the Forges de Buffon. As we arrived at the lock there, we seemed to be serenaded by an unseen accordion. Then, as we tied up, a diminutive figure appeared behind a huge accordion, playing a popular song – not very well, but recognizably. The player was nine years old and looked exactly like Shirley Temple, with a red spotted dress and curly fair hair. She had learnt to play the accordion at the local school in Montbard, where a professional lady accordionist taught on Wednesdays. The teacher had arrived in Montbard on some tour or other, had fallen madly in love with a chef, and settled down to start a restaurant with him. Their restaurant was very successful by all accounts, and her accordion lessons had produced the best young male accordionist in the all-European accordion championships. In Paris we had heard the great Marcel Adzola, who had been the accompanist for Edith Piaf, play quite superbly what must be the musical instrument of France. The accordion has set more moods – and in just a few bars – in French films and television than any other instrument. The little girl popped out with her accordion every time a tourist boat or hotel barge went by, hoping to get some money, which, of course, I gave her. I asked what she was going to do with it. Her mother could have done with the money, but this little girl said that she was going to buy a newer and better accordion. I hope she did.

The Forges de Buffon are, or rather were, where the Comte de Buffon manufactured a special steel from local ore. This is what stopped the guns of the French army blowing apart when larger and larger cannonballs were needed. The Swedes had the secret of an especially hard steel required in the manufacture of safe cannon barrels, but before Buffon found a similar mixture, the French had to put up with using only medium charges in their cannons, otherwise they would blow up, with great loss of life to those working the guns. Buffon was born in Montbard and had become one of the luminaries of eighteenth-century France and also keeper of the Jardin du Roi in Paris, after his learned thesis on natural history had been published. In four years he built these forges and diverted the local river, so that the water could be used to power the bellows for the forge and also the hammers required for beating out the red-hot metal. In the true spirit of eighteenth-century enlightenment, he had had a gallery built in the main area of the forge so that his guests, with their *jabots* and their jewels, could watch the wretched toilers as they worked in enormously high temperatures, tending the furnaces. The incentive to work in the furnace room was that you got extra rations and privileged accommodation. All this information was pumped at me by an incredibly energetic woman whose family had owned the place for the last eighty years or so. She spoke extremely good English, which was not surprising as she had married a charming but rather vague Englishman, who spent his days being supportive and perplexed by his wife's behaviour.

We had arrived, by pure chance, in the year that was the two hundredth anniversary of the death of Buffon, and to celebrate, this lady had decided to breed a hinnie. I had no idea what a hinnie was until she told me that it was a cross between a female donkey and a horse, or in this case a Welsh pony from the neighbouring farmer's fields. The great difference between a mule and a hinnie, she hectored me as though any fool should know, is that a hinnie can reproduce itself. I did my best to show that I was suitably impressed by this rare and extremely bad-tempered animal who, instead of nuzzling in the approved manner, chose to manoeuvre its hindquarters to let go a vicious kick. 'Oh you are naughty,' cried the owner, shooing the beast away. She was forced to repeat herself almost immediately as the loathsome hybrid turned on her, lashing out with a footballer's kick to the groin, which narrowly missed. What energy my guide had, what unstoppability: little wonder her husband had perfected the art of English vagueness.

CHAPTER EIGHT

Montbard to Mulhouse

Montbard is a pleasant old town of twisted roofs and moss-covered tiles, built on the side of a hill topped by a park which was once the site of a fortress. The Comte de Buffon is unquestionably Montbard's most famous former citizen by a long chalk. In the eighteenth century he had been the biggest employer in the area, using hundreds of men to collect fuel from the forests to heat his furnaces. He had employed women to build the park, paying them practically no money until they protested so vigorously that he agreed to pay them a little more. This setback would appear to have been the only reverse Buffon ever had to suffer in his life.

The canal at Montbard runs round the bottom of the town through a large basin. Here there were a number of hotel barges which left every few days, taking groups of passengers for trips up and down the Canal de Bourgogne. There was also a small harbour where a boat-hire company operated, as well as a berth or two for itinerants. All this looked a bit too clubby for us, so I decided to go through the first lock after the basin and tie up on the other side.

The charming young lock-lady there, who was in her twenties and had two small boys, allowed us to tie up just the other side of the lock and even provided us with water. When I asked her how long she thought she was going to be doing this job she replied that she would surely do it for the rest of her days, which she seemed very happy about. In this lock we were moored next to Montbard's main industry: a factory, still producing specialized steel, which it turned into tubes for nuclear reactors. The factory had just closed for the holiday and there was a feeling of excitement in the old streets as the children prepared for the torchlit procession that evening, and the older ones got themselves together for the *Grand Bal Gratuit* which Jacques Garcia, mayor for sixteen years, always laid on for the populace on the night before the glorious 14th of July.

Ray and I, feeling that we should enter into the spirit of the occasion, dressed the ship, which in our case meant getting all our signal flags out, joining them together in no particular order, and stretching them from the raised crane arm to the top of the stubby mast on the *Leo*. I have never been able to get the meaning of the signal flags straight, but I reasoned that, so far from the ocean, there would be very few seadogs about to correct the obvious mistakes that I am sure we must have made. We also festooned the boat with a garland of coloured lights and we were well pleased with the festive result. I went off to get some supplies from the local *charcutier* who said that in spite of it being a holiday he would be open on the morning of Bastille Day, and invited me to come to see his kitchen the next morning.

My son Jason and his girl Kate were arriving that evening from Paris, on one of France's TGVs (high-speed trains), which really do go buzzing along. I was very much looking forward to hearing Jason's traveller's tales, which were always punctuated with a good giggle or two. He duly arrived and introductions were made. Ray and the kids got on well from the start and we had a splendid march round the town in the *flambeaux* (torchlit) procession. This was led by the fire brigade and the Trompettes Montbardois – arguably the very worst band in the land. The mayor's daughter, who worked as her father's assistant in the town hall, confessed that the band were not up to playing the Marseillaise at the ceremony the next day, so they would have to play a record of France's anthem as the flag was raised. Outside the Hôtel de Ville we were handed coloured lanterns with candles inside, and set off with the crowd, marching round the town to the revolutionary beat of the drummers. The fire brigade had large flaming torches which had been dipped in kerosene and burned in a suitably flamboyant manner.

The procession wound its way round the town, the town louts throwing firecrackers to frighten the young and elderly, and finally arrived outside the hall where the *Grand Bal Gratuit* was taking place. The appalling band played a last – discordant – chord, and shambled off. The mayor explained that they normally had a live band from out of town for the *Grand Bal Gratuit*, but this year the town hall funds had been sadly depleted celebrating the bicentennial of the death of Buffon, and so the dance band had been cancelled.

We left the *bal* after a few minutes, as the music of Montbard was beginning to get us all down. We also had to be up very early the next day to enter Ray for the fishing competition, which was to take place a few yards from where the boat was moored.

Ray was duly entered and drew number 47, which was considered to be a good draw. There were about one hundred men and women in the competition, which took place, on a morning that was anything but glorious, in freezing drizzle. I walked with Ray to the stake that marked his spot and found next to it, as with all the others, a small pot of begonias. He had brought his short fishing rod, but it was clear that he was well out of his depth as all his fellow competitors unleashed huge carbon-fibre rods which stretched over eighteen feet into the middle of the canal. One of Ray's neighbours was a shortsighted gentleman who required an elderly pair of opera glasses to see his float, it was so far away. After an hour of serious fishing no one I saw had caught anything, and after a number of whispered conversations with the white hope of the *Leo*, we decided that he ought to change his bait from rolled-up balls of bread to red worms. These the lady on Ray's right kindly supplied – or was it a ploy? As soon as Ray had changed his bait the woman jerked her rod and pulled out a fish measuring a good three inches.

The mayor came up with a few asinine, vote-catching jokes about the fish not wanting to jump out of the canal, but since he had been mayor for the last sixteen summers, I expect the competitors were used to it. Ray decided that it just was not going to be his day, and left whistling the Marseillaise. I believe the winner won about three hundred pounds in prize money, which was about six hundred times more than the weight of the fish that he caught.

Jason, Kate and I went for our date with the *charcutier*, who showed us round the spotless kitchen where he was making large quantities of *pâté de campagne*, with pig's liver, lumps of white fat, buckets of garlic, and parsley. His kitchen looked out over the valley and I could see Ray on the *Leo* hundreds of feet below us. The *charcutier*, who sported the most magnificent moustache, explained that they bought a whole dead pig on a Friday, and used every single bit of it during the week, except the bones which they sold for fertilizer and glue. The delicious items that they had on show somehow did not look quite so appetizing after we'd seen and smelled the boiling cauldrons downstairs, and realized that the jelly which made the *langues de porc* look so good was from the pig's skin, rendered down over many hours. Hunger is the best cook, however, and by the time we had been to the ceremony at the Hôtel de Ville next door, we were all ready for what he had offered us.

The ceremony of the flag-raising went off well. The Trompettes gave a short, off-key blast on their instrument, the mayor's daughter turned on the gramophone, and we all stood to attention for the Marseillaise. The mayor made a speech with a lot of references to faith and hope, and then bestowed medals on the police and on the fire brigade (in France, the fire brigade seem to do everything that the police do not, including rushing people to hospital after emergencies of any kind). The star of the show was a pretty woman, a captain-doctor in the fire brigade, who seemed to be getting all the honours and a good deal of over-zealous, congratulatory kissing from the male brass. The gathering broke up and people drifted back to their homes for a good, solid meal before the afternoon's events, which were to be held in Buffon's park after everyone had digested their dinner, and included the *Grand Concours de Pétanque* and the *Vin d'Honneur*.

Ray and I decided to enter for the *pétanque* competition. Ray was drawn with a pretty neat couple of players and went off to one end of the park, and I became the handicap of a practically professional *pétanque* player, a wiry Algerian called Zappy. He soon saw that my standard was less than amateur and tried to show me a few tricks of the trade in the last minutes before the game. We lasted one round, thanks to the brilliance of Zappy, but he very kindly said that had I had professional *boules*, which were heavier, rather than the supermarket variety I was using, I would have made a much better show. The truth is that *pétanque* is a vicious game, and I was way out of my depth, both in my throwing skill and in the devious tactical gambits required. Ray and I have since spent many hours practising with professional *boules*. Perhaps one day we shall be asked to play again and make a better showing of ourselves.

The mayor and his daughter set up the tables and brought the bottles of Burgundy that had been promised, together with bottles of lemonade for the children, and once the last *boule* had been thrown the wine started to flow. The fire chief's daughter had just been promoted, which was an occasion for further fervent kissing. There is no doubt that when you are promoted in the fire service in Montbard you get more kisses if you are the fire chief's daughter and pretty as well; there is also no doubt that you get promoted. The crowds drank their glass of wine and wandered off down the hill into the town, and the crew of the *Leo* said farewell to their new-found friends and prepared for a morning departure. As we reached the barge our friend the *charcutier* appeared, bringing us a couple of bottles of wine for the journey and a special pâté. It looked delicious: our memories of the manu- facture had dwindled.

The last act of the day, and the last gathering, was for the *feux d'artifice*, the firework display, though this also suffered from the lack of funds resulting from the expense of Buffon's anniversary. The whole affair excited the firecracker throwers to such a frenzy that matters became quite unpleasant. I must confess that I do not like firecrackers. I was in Penang – the 'jewel of the Orient' – during the Malayan Emergency. The town had a large Chinese population, and a firecracker going off could mean that a bullet was on its way. On Christmas Eve 1953, I remember, it once meant just that – the pineapple plant under which I had thrown myself, on hearing what I thought was probably an exploding firecracker, was leaking juice.

Fireworks over, Montbard had had its holiday and the populace had had their dose of Revolution for another year. I very much hope this little town in Burgundy, bypassed by the motorways and the rest of France, goes on celebrating the fall of the Bastille for many centuries to come.

The four of us, Ray, Jason, Kate and I, said our adieus to our friendly lock-lady and set off, passing the site of the fishing contest where I distinctly saw some quite big fish jumping into the air in a mocking display. The countryside became more and more remote as, mounting through at least twenty locks in quick succession, we reached the battlefields of Alesia where Julius Caesar conquered the Gauls in AD 52. It was interesting to see how the Romans, holding the high ground, must have swooped down on their enemies and routed them. No doubt it was soon after the battle that they established the vineyards at Pouilly. For us, Pouilly was the summit level

137

– and that usually meant there was a tunnel; here it was over three kilometres long. The reason that tunnels are constructed at summits is that with rising series of locks it's necessary to be able to build a reservoir above the canal level in order to replenish it with water when the locks are opened: near a summit, where there's no more room for an above-canal reservoir, a tunnel must be built. This tunnel was very deceptive: the entrance was larger than the middle, and we ended up having to take down all our awnings and aerials to pass through. In the old days, unladen barges would be put into a tank barge, which would then be sunk and the whole rig towed through by a winch at the end.

It was very dark in the tunnel, and the noise from the engine was deafening. Our searchlight picked out many clusters of bats minding their own business on the brick-lined roof. What a work of construction the canal must have been! It was once the main route for the wine transporters from Beaune, and until the Canal de la Marne à la Saône and the Canal du Centre were built, the way through for Paris-bound barges from the South.

Our leisurely descent through Burgundy was full of incident. I had been drying some clothes in the tumble-dryer and had forgotten to open the front hatch to let out the steam. I tried to push it from the inside, but when I had it half-open my hand slipped on the condensation, bringing the heavy steel frame crashing down on my finger. My nail was crushed. Later that day, Ray found the blow-lamp and we heated up a needle and pierced the nail to allow the pressurized blood to ooze out and stop the throbbing.

Jason and I decided that, to cheer me up, we should open the barrel of wine that we had loaded on in Paris. Because of the lack of space on the barge, I decided to put the wine into plastic containers, thinking that it would not be around for long. We lifted the barrel on to the deck and then made

138

the mistake that everyone unfamiliar with barrels makes. We knocked out the plug and pushed the tap in, then laid the barrel down on its side. Nothing came out, of course, because there was an air lock inside the barrel. We heaved and laid it on its side again, and removed the main filling bung which is situated on the side of the barrel. This released the air lock but unfortunately we had put the tap in so that it was now facing upwards. The only thing to do was to put the main bung back in, pull out the tap, and start all over again. By the time we had finished the operation we all felt that, even if we did not deserve a drink, we needed one. I realized that it was not really on to be drinking Bordeaux in Burgundy, but felt our palates needed to be able to compare the bouquets.

Ray and I would take turns to ride the bike along to the next lock and prepare for the *Leo*'s arrival, while Jason and Kate took over the catering and produced one gourmet meal after another – requiring the maximum amount of exercise to work off the extra calories. The raw materials in this region simply taste better than supermarket food, though the cooking by the London foodies on board enhanced its qualities. Lock-keepers offered us cassis, lettuces, chickens and every other home-grown, home-made delicacy available, but never mustard which, so close to Dijon, I had thought they would all make.

What with the beautiful weather, the ripening corn fields, the backlit châteaux perched on the top of the hills, this was indeed '*la vie en rose*'. We soon got into the rhythm of a lunchtime picnic on the banks, and early bedtimes. One day we arrived at a lock just as a pleasure boat was leaving it, and as we entered an enormous carp leapt out of the water and landed on the quay. It must have weighed at least twenty pounds, but the lock-keeper insisted that, as we had picked it up, we should keep it. We gave him a bottle of Scotch and proceeded to cut up the fish. As we did so, we found that the pleasure boat's propeller had damaged its tail fin.

Apparently carp, when they know they have a wound from which they will not recover, prefer to commit suicide by leaping on to the bank with their last strength. Knowing this, none of us wanted to eat it, so we walked along to the hotel barge next door, which was run by an Englishman from the North, and gave the great fish to him. He took one look at it and suggested that he could serve it up as turbot to the new intake of guests that had just arrived. I must say I felt a little sorry for the passengers, but they were clearly there to enjoy themselves and carp served up as turbot, in French, was not going to bother them one bit.

The *Leo* seemed to have joined the mood of the party and was working perfectly, and we soon reached Dijon. To my surprise, everyone on board voiced their unspoken thoughts and begged me not to stop in the hot and noisy town, but to press on into the country. As it happened, I knew an ideal spot about a day's journey from the town where I had been years before with my younger daughter, Sabine. The weather had become extremely warm, so it was very pleasant to stop for a few days in the cool, clear waters of the Saône, a little upstream of St-Jean-de-Losne. We unloaded the car for shopping and for visiting, and moored up in this delightful place.

On one of the days of our stay, I took the car to visit the vineyards in Vosne Romanée. When I arrived in the village I parked the car, walked round, and discovered a sign made in the shape of a vineleaf with the name of the proprietor, Sylvian Cathiard, on it. M. Cathiard was washing bottles in his outhouse with a metal gadget which scrubbed the inside, leaving no trace of sediment. Mme Cathiard was stacking the clean bottles in crates and picking the paper off the ones that had to be washed. Their ten-year-old son ran about chasing imaginary robbers.

The Cathiards described their establishment to me in stereo, because M. Cathiard had an extreme stutter and his wife kept stepping in to explain and amplify what he was saying. They were managing some vines that belonged to the woman's family, and they had hopes of finally inheriting them. They also rented some vines which they worked, giving half the produce to the owners, a positively feudal system but one that suited them very well because they were not likely to be ruined by a disastrous harvest. They produced about ten thousand bottles a year for which they did all the work. They both had to work exceptionally hard, but as M. Cathiard stuttered, 'We love our work and we work with passion.' Their most expensive wine came from the in-laws' vines and cost about one hundred francs a bottle, but it would not be considered drinkable for at least another ten years. If wine takes on the character of the vintner, the Cathiards' produce must be a good buy. I very much hope that some greedy bank does not foreclose on them, for they are very proud of what they do, and, somehow, barring accidents, I believe they will succeed.

It was hard to tear ourselves away from the idle way of life we had established under the spreading oak tree beside the river. There was a good deal of swimming and fishing, and the contents of the barrel of wine, now in its plastic containers, was all too soon disposed of. But the *Sylphe* – the barge we had passed in Paris – had caught us up, and I decided it was a good thing to follow reasonably close behind him, so that he would churn up the bottom of the canal and make it easier for us: it was the dry season and there was very little water in the canals.

As we made our way up the Doubs valley the countryside began to change from the lushness of Burgundy to rather more rugged terrain. When we reached Dole we stopped to take on some water, and as we did a troop of boy scouts came and asked us whether we were going to Besançon. We said we were, but that it might take quite a while. They were concerned that their rivals in the initiative test, the Squirrel troop, might pip them to the post. I decided I would take them, and, if they worked hard at the locks, buy them tickets on the train from wherever we were to Besançon. The scouts were nice boys from Dunkerque and immediately fell in love with Kate, who fed them and stuffed provisions into their haversacks in a motherly way, which made me think of Wendy and the lost boys in *Peter Pan*. The boys told Jason that they had all won badges for making *kir royale* (champagne and cassis) and cooking *coq au vin*. What else does a young Frenchman need to know?

They sat on the bows as we went through some of the most seductive country on the trip so far, with high white granite cliffs and wooded hills, and sang scout songs about the river of life, which seemed appropriate. Towards the evening we came to a small town where there appeared to be a railway station, and we put the boys ashore with enough cash for a ticket. I was impressed by the way they went about things and hoped they would get to Besançon before the Squirrel patrol.

As we followed the *Sylphe* up the Doubs river, we found that a moment's inattention would run the head of the barge on to a bank. When this happened, we had to spend time backing off, and in some cases had to detach the *Leo* altogether and take her into deeper water to drag the barge off the banks sideways. While we had charts, the river is not buoyed and the silting occurs very rapidly – something the charts are ready to admit. We had to proceed very slowly in any case, as the *Sylphe* was creeping along in front of us, and it is *de rigueur* to stay behind a working barge in these conditions. Pleasure boats are constantly trying to overtake these lumbering barges and fail to understand why the *bateliers* are so resentful. The fact is they plan their journeys down to the last minute of lock opening times, only to have their schedule disrupted by some selfish yachtsman who merely wants to get to the nearest marina for a bath.

The citadel at Besançon towered above the river as we approached the old town. We moored in the centre of the city next to a very lively market that sold everything from carrots to antique lace. On the way into the town we had to follow a work boat through the shallow canal, and passed the cleverest piece of mooring that I have ever seen. The lower walls of the citadel rise sheer from the water's edge at one point, and the only crevices in the face of the wall are archers' slits. Through one of these some clever sailor had slipped a grappling hook on the end of a rope and secured his vessel.

Near our mooring was a small square where two plaques commemorated the fact that this little corner of France was the birthplace of two of the giants of the nineteenth century. On the southern side the great novelist Victor Hugo, recently enjoying a burst of publicity because his saga *Les Misérables* seems to have become the world's most success-ful musical, has the letters of his name picked out in gold. On the western side the brothers Lumière, fathers of modern cinema, have a dual plaque recalling their achievements. It is most extraordinary that these three men should have started their lives within a few years of each other, and within hailing distance, in this small town. I wondered who had the most influence on the inhabitants of Besançon today.

We went on up the Doubs, fouling the propeller frequently, until we reached a plain near the summit from which we would be descending into the valley of the Rhine. As we went through one lock in the middle of nowhere, a party of really pretty children asked if they could have a lift to the next lock along. They jumped aboard and during the short trip they told me that their parents had just got married. When we arrived at the lock there was the woman, who must have weighed twenty stone if she weighed an ounce, and her husband who was exactly the opposite: a small scrawny man wearing a T-shirt proclaiming that he was in the 'Big Rigs Club' – something to do with heavy lorries, I believe. The wedding had been the day before but the dogs all had

143

white bows around their necks, and everyone was still in an extremely festive mood.

They decided that they should celebrate further by having a little adventure on board the *Leo*. I can remember the look of astonishment on Ray's face when they all got on and presented us with a large bucket of cut flowers left over from the wedding. Chatting to them, I discovered that they had both been married before but had been left by their spouses with all the children. They had produced a little boy themselves and were now getting married to put their house in order. He worked in the local automobile plant and his fellow workers had given him a wedding present, some sort of gadget for his car, of which he was very proud. She was so very large and had such a sweet nature, her children were so attractive, and they all so clearly adored each other that we were sad to see them leave. The parting ended in hysterics as the quay of the lock was about six feet above the deck of the barge, which meant that the large lady had to be pushed up the ladder to fall forward and roll in a giggling heap on the top. We waved adieu to this jolly family and started our descent into Germany.

In a sense the holidays were over. Jason and Kate departed, leaving the larder well stocked, and Ray and I set off in the morning mist, down a flight of thirteen locks, to the approaches of Mulhouse. On the way we passed a tribe of German yachtsmen bound for the Mediterranean. German yachtsmen tend to travel in packs when they venture outside Germany, with a group leader and rigid timetables, much to the consternation of French lock-keepers. The countryside had started to assume subtle signs of the Black Forest, which lay about fifty miles to the east, on the other side of the Rhine. The eaves of the houses were becoming more sloped and there were stacks of firewood outside nearly all the cottages. We were in Alsace-Lorraine and before long reached Mulhouse; we were about to face the first serious bureaucratic problem of our voyage. The captain of the *Sylphe* had told me how tough it was for him to go on the Rhine, but I was hoping that the jolly, innocent-British-yachtsman line would work. I had an unwelcome surprise in store.

CHAPTER NINE
Mulhouse to Mannheim

Our first taste of Mulhouse was of that rare thing – an unpleasant lock-keeper. He refused to let us through his lock so we could spend the night in the town, even though we had arrived fifteen minutes before lock closing time. He clearly thought we needed a bit of discipline having only been in touch with country bumpkins on our way through from Paris, and gave us his version of the rules about mooring. He earned the honour of being the only lock-keeper of a manual lock in all France to whom I did not give the customary *pourboire*, or tip. I normally donated ten francs towards the family finances and sometimes more if the weather was particularly beastly. I do not think the government pay them very much and goodwill spreads like wildfire down the line if a reasonably pleasant rapport is established at the entry to a canal.

To get our own back on this growling curmudgeon, we announced our departure for half past six in the morning, when the locks opened. For some reason quite beyond me, he then became extremely affable, had the lock all ready before the opening time, and was all smiles. I shall never fathom why his attitude towards us changed so rapidly. Perhaps his father had an unpleasant experience with the British during the war.

I had heard, of course, that we would have to get papers for our trip down the Rhine, and Mulhouse seemed the appropriate place to sort things out. In rough terms, any boat displacing more than fifteen tons of water has to have a licence to travel down the Rhine, and the captain of the vessel has to be licensed to steer the ship. This meant, as the captain of the *Sylphe* had told me, knowing where to anchor in a dense fog, if all that could be seen were the kilometre posts on the banks. You also had to prove that you had completed sixteen journeys up and down the Rhine as an assistant. Suddenly we were into the big stuff, and it was like being on the Thames again. We were through the last Freycinet-size lock of the journey and the width of the canal had quadrupled in size. How sad it will be when this large canal is extended the way we had just come, down the beautiful valley of the Doubs to link the Rhine to the Mediterranean via the Rhône. I am afraid that, commercial reasons aside, it will be an environmental disaster.

We stopped at around midday in an odd place called the Île Napoléon, which seemed to be the mosquito capital of Europe. There was a marina there run by an old river man called Jacob. He knew what the rules were, but our unorthodox craft made him suck his teeth a bit. We already knew that we would have to get a signalling board, which has replaced the blue-flag system. On the Rhine a ship coming up against the swift current has the right to choose its passage. If the captain wants to pass starboard to starboard (the wrong way), he puts up his blue board and the ship going downstream has to acknowledge the manoeuvre by displaying their own. The ships then pass blue board to blue board.

At this mooring were half a dozen waiting French barges. I asked M. Jacob why they were there, and he told me they were all waiting for permits to take their craft on the Rhine, and that they, like us, would first have to get a pilot. Slowly the awful truth began to dawn on us that there would be someone else on board. The inspector for all these boats was due that very afternoon, so we collected the blue board that M. Jacob conveniently had in stock, and tidied up the *Leo* ready for the inspection. I talked to our neighbours on the commercial barges and they told me that the inspector who was coming was a real terror. Ray was getting very hot and

147

bothered about the idea of having to have a pilot and I was very anxious about the unorthodox way the boats were coupled together.

When the inspector arrived, he and Jacob had a quick conference which I was sure was significant. Then he started on us, and I must say he was thorough, very thorough. He looked at everything, from the anchor chain to the stern gland, and then went off, announcing that he would be back in an hour after he had given one of the other barges a good going over. Ray was incensed: we had come all the way from London and across the Channel without the slightest sniff of an inspection, and now, when we were about to go one way down a wide river, our boat might be pronounced unseaworthy, and, whatever the outcome, we would have to employ a pilot.

On his return the inspector, who obviously had had another chat with Jacob, came and told us what his verdict was. He told us that the Rhine Commission were very tough and that, with luck, he might be able to persuade them to give us a permit to make one trip, providing that we doubled up on the coupling holding the two boats together. This was not a problem, but then came the crunch. He said that the Commission would have no alternative but to consider us a convoy, and bound by the rules that applied to convoys of ten to fifteen thousand tons. To our horror he then calculated that on the stern of the *Leo* we would need a two-hundred-kilogramme anchor with a huge winch, to drop in case of emergency. When I told Ray he just laughed, but the inspector looked very stern and said that those were the rules, that he was bending over backwards to help, and all the usual jargon that officials use when they are trying to explain the ludicrous. I had to accept what he said, and also the suggestion that Jacob might be able to help us out. When I agreed to see Jacob, the inspector said that, while he could not officially allow us to go down the Grand Canal d'Alsace without the necessary permits, he would turn a blind eye –

if we turned up in Strasbourg for a final inspection before he gave us the clearance for the Rhine proper. I felt duly grateful and then wondered why: it all seemed a bit unreasonable, but since neither of us had ever been on the Rhine it was just possible that it lived up to its name of the 'Rhin sauvage'.

Imagine our surprise when Jacob said that he had just the size anchor and winch and just the amount of chain that we now required. Ray, with the cunning of a London river man, was convinced that all this was a 'stitch-up', but I prepared for the worst: this monstrous impediment that we would now have hanging on the stern of the poor old *Leo* was going to cost five hundred pounds. The anchor would take a day to arrive from Strasbourg, where I am sure Jacob had a friend whose business it was to break barges up for scrap, so Ray and I decided to go and have a look at the French Railway Museum.

The SNCF are a vastly powerful and efficient body in France. The service they offer is a model of how a railway should be run, and the same can be said of their railway museum. It is extremely well housed, in a disused railway shed on the outskirts of Mulhouse, and had grown considerably since the last time I was there, when we were doing research for the film of Agatha Christie's *Murder on the Orient Express*. The superb rolling stock of the Wagon-Lit company was gleaming, and since there were not many people about, I asked the curator whether I might have the carriages opened so that I could show Ray some of the features of the construction. When we had made the film, I had bought a complete *wagon-lit* carriage from the breaker's yard, sold back the bogey, and transported the top half to the studios where it was reassembled by a Belgian specialist. When the film came to an end I kept all the pieces, and in fact used some of the specially toughened glass windows in the interior of the barge. The care with which these carriages were built is quite astonishing by today's standards. All the metal fittings were

149

cast brass, with a dull chrome finish that would be prohibi-
tively expensive to duplicate today. The train was entirely
first class, and each compartment had its own washing
cupboard. The splashplates on the doors of these cupboards
were made from real sharkskin, with the roughness carefully
sandpapered off so it did not catch on your legs. Plastic is
much more practical no doubt, but somehow I have never
felt frightened of sharks since I learned that their skins could
be used in this way.

I can remember travelling on the famous Blue Train from
Marseilles to Paris with my mother and sister. My mother
had not wanted to travel through the Bay of Biscay and had
disembarked from the P&O ship on the way back to England.
The excitement of walking through the slightly swaying
corridors, past the conductor warming himself by his little
coal stove, and on to the dining car, is with me still. The
dining cars in the museum are the ultimate in design for a
travel environment. Built in the late thirties, all the glass
panels were made by the Lalique glass company, using their
famous ground-glass effect. Slim nymphs were everywhere,
gazing into pools or holding up lampshades. The tables in
the restaurant were all laid with that special chunky, plated
cutlery, the famous WL logo engraved on the handles, which
I had such difficulty in lifting as a child.

Ray and I sat in the compartment while the public filed
past the windows; the raised platform outside had a switch
in the floor which automatically turned the compartment
lights on as they went by. I told Ray of how, when John
Brabourne, my partner, and I were raising the money for
Orient Express, we had gone to see Charlie Bludhorn, the
financial wizard who had bought Paramount Pictures. We
did not expect him to have heard of the railway, but we were
in for a surprise. Ensconced in an incredibly expensive office
on top of his fifty-five-storey skyscraper in New York, this
czar of all he surveyed scoffed, and said that he remembered
the glamour of the train very well – from the days when it

Dressed over all for Bastille Day, Montbard.

A young accordionist . . .

and admirers.

A perfect place in Burgundy – where we opened our barrel of Bordeaux!

At summit-level in the Doubs.

A good mooring in Strasbourg.

used to come through the station at Vienna when he had been a waiter there. He gave us the money to make the film, which was an astute move and very fortunate for us.

The next day dawned to a heavy drizzle – not exactly what we would have ordered to do our fixing of the winch and anchor. The latter arrived swinging from the bucket of a mechanical digger, and was greeted by a look of incredulity from Ray. When we loaded it all on, with the required thirty metres of chain, the stern of the *Leo* sank about four inches in the water. We had to rummage about in the storage area under the afterdeck and take everything off the boat on to the barge to improve the situation. We were able to halve the amount the stern had sunk, but even so the boat was too low for anything but the calmest waters. We had complied with the regulations, however, so we parted with the five hundred pounds and made ready to set off again for the Grand Canal d'Alsace, along the branch canal that runs to it from Mulhouse.

The Grand Canal itself runs north from Strasbourg and very nearly reaches Basel, in Switzerland. Basel, surprisingly, is the port with the second highest tonnage figure in Europe. As soon as we were through the giant lock into the main canal we could see why. There was a procession of very large barges churning up and down, much faster than we could ever move. The barges had two, sometimes three crews, and ran non-stop from destination to destination. They usually took four days from Rotterdam to Basel against the current, and two days going the other way. All the locks were prepared for their arrival, which they announced over their radios, and it was very rare to see a barge waiting for a lock to open. This created a new problem for us: all the lock-keepers spoke German, and very quickly at that. We just had to wait till the commercial barges had gone into the lock and nip in behind them, hoping that the lock-keeper did not close his massive gates on the *Leo* and crush her to pulp.

151

They never did, of course, but I was glad when we finally reached Strasbourg on the evening of the next day.

'Strasbourg – France's gateway on the Rhine' announced a large placard as we crept into the city on a lovely golden evening: past the parliament for the European Community and on into the centre of the town, where we tied up alongside the Quai des Pêcheurs, who have long since ceased to ply their trade from here. All we had to do now was to wait for the Rhine inspector to come and inspect the wart that had grown on our stern. The restriction of having to wait for permission was something that had not happened to us before, and it was very annoying. Ray and I decided to cross the Quai des Pêcheurs and have a drink in a lively bar where the students of Strasbourg University were having an end-of-year farewell party. They drank too much, we drank too much, the songs were blue, and though we did not understand the words, the sense was clear enough. We were glad it was only a short walk back to the barge.

The inspector called the following morning and said the work looked satisfactory. All he had to do now was to convince the authorities that they should allow us to have our one-way permission. I felt that the battle was over and it was now only a matter of time before we were on our way again. The inspector had told us that we could moor here, but the authorities wanted us to move on. I decided that, while this might be a poor trump card, I could at least say that since we did not have the permission, we could not move. I explained all this to the inspector and told him that he had better get his colleagues to hurry up with their weighty decision.

There were pleasure boats taking rides round the canals, so we decided to go on one. It was exactly the same as a pleasure trip anywhere else, with instantly forgettable facts being shouted through a loudspeaker. Ray and I preferred to look at what interested us rather than listen to all this indigestible information. I did notice a rather pleasant-looking family who had their home in the bottom part of a building right on the edge of the canal. I resolved to try to find out where they lived and call on them to find out what they did. After our busman's holiday I walked down the street where I thought their house should be. I asked a gentleman who was getting out of his car if he could help. It turned out that he was a Lutheran pastor who, because of an odd series of coincidences, had been drafted into one of the more bizarre forms of the ministry to which he belonged: being a Protestant, he spoke both German and French and had been chosen to be the Padre at Spandau Prison. He had worked there for five years in the early fifties, when the seven famous Nazi war criminals were incarcerated there. None of them, he said, showed the slightest remorse – except for Raeder who told him that he had given Pastor Niemöller the chance to escape. Niemöller had been a naval commander in the First World War, and Raeder told him he could leave Dachau provided he stopped all protest against the Nazi regime. The Pastor, a very brave man, refused – and spent the rest of the war in the concentration camp. The Padre also told me that it was the Americans who first gave the prisoners turkey for Christmas, in 1950, the fourth Christmas that they had been there. It must have been an odd job to be in charge of the spiritual needs of these men.

The Pastor told me how to reach the house which I had seen from the canal. I went and talked to the family there, who told me that their modern home, with its balcony over-looking the canal, had been an old garage which they had converted. The father's trade was very high-quality litho-graphic printing, and he took me out to see his works on an industrial estate on the outskirts of Strasbourg. Artists and painters came and worked with him to manufacture prints of their work. This was what he specialized in, though he had to earn the rent by printing advertisements for the usual inanities. I found his large facsimile of the original design for Strasbourg Cathedral quite fascinating. The detail that the draughtsman of four hundred years or so ago had put into the plan was quite extraordinary. Strasbourg Cathedral, as the design showed, should have had two spires, but when they came to build the southern spire the foundations began to sink. The front of the cathedral is so ornate that one rarely looks up to see that there is a missing spire. Where the spire should have been, two hundred feet above the street, someone has built a postcard kiosk, which looks quite grotesque perched high over the town like that, though perhaps its earnings keep the roof in good repair.

Once a year Strasbourg has a market in the heart of the city, which is completely closed to traffic for the day. Thousands of people come from all over the area. Gypsies, Algerians, Turks from across the Rhine in Germany, and representatives of every other nationality under the sun. The crowded medieval city had the feeling of how I imagine the famous fairs of the middle ages to have been, with throngs of wide-eyed people genuinely amazed by what they were seeing. It is very sad to see so little wonder in people's eyes these days, but I suppose it's because everyone thinks they have seen everything there is to see on the television. Voyaging slowly on the *Leo*, one felt every nuance of the change in the countryside, every tiny influence of the changing population and their habits. Outside in the open, the weather, too, had a very strong bearing on how one felt about a place. This physical involvement, the air round the people and places, is the essence of travelling and something that cannot be substituted.

Monday morning again. We were still waiting for the Rhine inspector to return with the papers, and, worse still, the name of a suitable pilot for our descent of the *Rhin sauvage* once, two or three locks downstream, it was flowing freely, uncorseted by canalization. The papers finally arrived in the afternoon and we had a clean bill of health from the Commission, whoever they were. There is a British representative on this commission, which is considered a sinecure by

154

the French as there is precious little British involvement in shipping on the Rhine. Our inspector had put on a gaily coloured shirt and I suppose, like all prisoners and their captors, we had grown quite fond of this meticulous man with his rules and calculations. He had the grace to admit that these had been mistaken by 25 per cent in regard to the size of the anchor. Ray and I looked at each other, thinking that this mistake might have been made because that was the only anchor that Jacob had had in stock at the time, but that was an ungallant thought. There was nothing to do but grin and bear it, and hope that we would never have to drop the anchor in anger, because if we did there was a very good chance that the poor old *Leo* would be pulled in half like some saint in Foxe's *Book of Martyrs*.

Our pilot followed close on the heels of the departing inspector. He was a small French *batelier* who spoke German and lived in Strasbourg Harbour on his barge, which was too small to make much money with. He supplemented his income by piloting French barges, and the odd voyager like ourselves, up and down the Rhine. He came to us through an agent, so he must have been quite well known. His fee was fifty pounds a day plus travelling expenses, and we arranged to start from the harbour at six thirty the following morning. Ray was, by this time, quite rightly feeling that the pilot's arrival was an unnecessary expense, and had taken a dislike to the man. I could see that I was going to have to dance about a bit to keep tempers from fraying. Luckily my younger daughter Sabine and her boyfriend Robert, returning from a youth orchestra concert in the South of France where they had both been playing the violin, were due to arrive that evening. I hoped that this would cause a distraction for Ray, and take his mind off the vagaries of the EEC bureaucracy.

The following morning we were all up at 0.600 hours. Shipshape and Bristol fashion – as much as we ever could be – we left the centre of Strasbourg for the harbour, to pick up the pilot and to tackle the much vaunted *Rhin sauvage*. He was there waiting for us, carrying a small holdall, which seems to be the sign of all boat people everywhere. We discovered later that he lived on little packets of soup that were dissolved in boiling water. He never ate or drank anything else, except water. I found Ray trying to explain that when you put the *Leo* astern, she always cut to port. The pilot was not listening: he was one of those men who knew how to do everything better than anyone else.

For the first couple of hours all went well, as we were still on the canalized section of the Rhine. In the penultimate lock I took a ride with a family of three – a Dutchman, his wife and their small son who was just home from school for the summer holidays. They owned what seemed like a vast barge, though by Rhine standards it was small, being a mere 1300 tons. They managed this monster on their own, and were planning to be in Holland in a couple of days, even though they had chipped their propeller and were getting a certain amount of vibration as they pushed along with their load of gravel for Rotterdam. I was proudly shown over their spotless barge, which was called the *Janna*. They had a large saloon with washing and drying machines, a bridge you could have got lost in, a television and a video machine, two bedrooms, and a bathroom. It was their home and they had to work very hard to keep it going. They had a radio telephone which kept them in touch with their freight bureau all the time, so they were able to accept cargoes from wherever they were. The system on the Rhine for making phone calls over the ship's VHF system is very efficient. The Dutch couple said that they did not make a fortune, but were able to keep going. They were very proud of their skill; the wife had all the same permits to drive this great ship as her husband did, so they could go for days and nights without stopping if they had to. They told me that they could have made a lot more money if they had had a bigger barge, but that would have necessitated employing crew, which would have meant all sorts of extra problems, so they were happy to stay as they were. The amount of time that they had to wait between voyages was considerably less than their colleagues in the rest of Europe – with the exception of the Germans and the Swiss.

The *Janna* had been much swifter than the *Leo* and I had to wait for a while on the last lock before the real Rhine. I found myself wondering how Ray and the pilot were getting on, and could imagine Ray watching and waiting for the poor man to make a mistake. While I was there a Swiss tow of 15,000 tons inched its way into the lock, with no more than six inches to spare on either side of the barges. A huge pusher unit was manoeuvring them gradually into the lock from behind. The size of these tows may not come near to the size of the ones on the Mississippi – but they were enormous compared with what we had been used to.

The *Leo* turned up and I had a briefing from Sabine, a veteran of many voyages on the *Leo*, about Ray and the pilot. She said that Ray was not at all happy and thought it very unfair that his command had been taken away from him. I could only agree, but we were entering the Rhine proper after this lock and if the pilot was to be of any use it would be now. For the first few miles the river was indistinguishable from the canalized river that we had been on. Then it became much narrower and we found ourselves putting up our blue board to pass a convoy of upstream barges starboard to starboard. This was not particularly exciting in itself, but the pilot and Ray now had something to do together which reduced the hostile atmosphere. I looked up to see the German customs post go flashing past, and frantically signalled to the pilot that we had to stop there. As I did so there was a great blast of 'achtungs' from the loudspeaker on the customs pontoon telling us to stop at once. This was not so easy because as we turned round we were swept further downstream and it took us about half an hour to turn and push our way back up to the customs house. As we did so a smart

157

green customs launch, which had been radioed to come and make sure we did not do a runner, arrived alongside and asked for our papers. The procedure was simple and efficient but it was the first time that I had been confronted with Germans who spoke only German, and as mine was woefully rusty, I began to realize that it was going to be much harder to make myself understood in future. Up went our courtesy flag and we were into Germany.

The first thing we noticed was the very large number of mobile bridge craft. I think that the NATO forces were about to make one of their periodic exercises to cross the Rhine, for there were American and German soldiers everywhere, whizzing about in inflatable boats and getting their huge lorries stuck in the marshy areas on the banks. We had our first taste of what we later called the German stare. The soldiers, or whatever they were, circled the *Leo* in their speedboats and gazed implacably at us with dead fish eyes, but the strong current had us whizzing along and we were soon in Speyer where I had said we would stop to buy some provisions.

As the pilot made to chuck round to come head up into the stream so that we could land at Speyer, he swung right out towards the far bank to make his turn. The river had created some new sandbanks which he was not expecting, and I could see Ray brighten visibly as the bows of the barge went firmly aground. The pilot then went astern and drove the stern of the *Leo* straight on to another sandbank. Ray and I had been in the same fix a number of times, and we knew that the only way out of it was to detach the *Leo* from the barge, free her from the sand and then lay off a hundred yards or so in deeper water and haul the barge off the bank backwards.

The sheer bliss of *Schadenfreude* had Ray beaming and I went astern to tell the pilot what he should do. He ignored me at first as he drove the poor old *Leo* forwards and back embedding her further at each attempt. Finally I got annoyed

158

and told him that Ray and I were going to drop the anchor on the barge whether he liked it or not and then detach the *Leo*. I don't think he believed that we would be so insubordinate but soon realized we meant what we said. I went forward again and dropped the anchor while Ray released the *Leo* from the barge. The pilot was going astern at the time and shot backwards as the tug was released and got firmly stuck in the sandbank. He realized at this moment that we were in charge. Gradually he got himself off, we threw him a rope from the barge and the rest of the operation went smoothly. The barge was anchored in deep water while we reattached the *Leo*, and off we went again without getting our provisions. It seemed that the pilot had another ship to take up the river that evening and they were waiting for him at Mannheim.

Within the hour we were approaching this industrial city. What city in Germany is not industrial in some way? The pilot wanted to be dropped off for his next job. Ray took over the tiller, happy to be back in charge of the boat once more. With incredible skill he turned the rig in the strong current and brought us up to within two feet of the barges our pilot was to take up river that evening. The pilot stepped aboard, and after a hurried conversation shouted out that the barges had broken down and he was going to have to mend them himself. By this time Ray had turned round again and we were way out of earshot. We would be seeing him in a few days after we had gone up to Heidelberg, and planned to meet him in Mannheim when we came through again.

Ray and I, plus Sabine and Robert, were suddenly free and covered the last few miles rapidly, through Mannheim where we turned right into the Neckar. We tied up on a pleasure-boat pier that was clearly not in use and walked up the bank into the town. The main tram depot greeted us when we got to the top and because we were tired we decided to go to the closest restaurant which turned out to be a Chinese. It was

159

not quite what I had planned for Sabine's first night in Germany, but, as ever, hunger is the best cook and I remember eating well before we turned in.

CHAPTER TEN

Mannheim to Frankfurt

It only took about two hours to make our way from Mannheim to Heidelberg. It is hard for me to think of Heidelberg without thinking of *The Student Prince*, of which I have very special memories. When I lived in the smart part of London, in Belgravia, we had a very small cinema theatre in our basement where we could run 16mm films. I had a friend who was a great fan of Ramon Novarro and he had been approached by the secretary of the Ramon Novarro fan club – whose membership had dwindled to five ladies and a gentleman – to run the film of *The Student Prince* in which Novarro had starred. In those days it was extremely hard to get prints of old films and we had to ask a famous film historian to lend us his bootleg copy. When the fan club left after the showing of the film, there were a number of tear-soaked tissues under the seats. They probably thought it was the last time they would ever see their hero. They must have all been teenagers when they had joined the club, and the secretary had been the secretary when Novarro was alive. The idea of a member of royalty slumming it with the plebs and falling in love with a commoner has always been appealing to the masses and is, in fact, what keeps most of the British and French tabloids going today. Heidelberg University has, for the most part, been moved out of town, and all that is left now is a building that purports to be the *Gasthaus* where the student prince spent those heady and formative days.

The town of Heidelberg was well kept and neat, with a population of citizens who seemed to be concerned only with

161

obeying the rules. Ray and I lifted the car off to tour the town. We drove up to the castle and managed to get a fistful of parking tickets, which must be filling up a disk somewhere on somebody's computer. In the forecourt of the castle a company that puts on an annual performance was having their dress rehearsal for *The Student Prince* – in English. I became curious as to who these enthusiasts could be, and asked a girl at the back of the audience who was lounging against a tree. It appeared that most of the cast were from the nearby American Air Force base. The soprano was a chunky girl from California with a complexion like a peach which ripened visibly when, at the end of the 'Drinking Song', the students hoisted her to their shoulders for the final chorus and she began to slip inexorably from their grasp. I hope it went well on the night, but for now she ended in an embarrassed heap at the students' feet.

Our mooring in Heidelberg was close to the oldest part of the town, very near the town hall, in the reception lobby of which there happened to be a display of books about Israel. It seemed odd to have such an exhibition in a town like this, and I asked the pleasant-looking woman who seemed to be in charge what it was like to be a Jew in Germany in these days. She told me that she came from an Israeli family that had always lived in Israel and while still in Israel had married an Israeli whose mother had been German. Fifteen years previously they had come to Berlin where, before the war, many thousands of Jews had lived; now there were only a handful. When she had started, running a small newsagent's shop with her husband, she found it very hard indeed to like the country or the inhabitants, but time had passed and the local people had eventually come to her for their papers rather than the other *Ausländer* round the corner, who was a Turk. She had obviously made a success of her life in Germany and told me that when she arrived she was an Israeli, but now she felt like a Jew. While a few people came to browse through the books, she told me that when she had

162

first arrived, she had seen any man who was the right age and who could have been in the war as a possible murderer of her race. Now, she said, she had grown comfortable in Germany, but could never like it. I longed to ask why she did not leave but her sad eyes warned me to go no further.

Before we left Heidelberg we stopped for water at the local yacht club, which was just what a German yacht club should be, with a lot of retired gentlemen eager to share a beer at ten in the morning. Next to us was another visitor who was amused by this attention from the members, and, as I could see that he had a twinkle in his eye, I went to talk to him. He and his wife, who, he explained, was single-handedly supporting the German Post Office by at least fifty postcards every day, had been up the Rhine to Basel from their home port of Rotterdam. Being a Dutchman he spoke beautiful English in a direct manner, and told us that, before retirement, he'd been in charge of a huge Dutch firm building supertankers. In his youth he had been a racing yachtsman and had been in famous boats before the war, when the Dutch were at the top of the league in twelve-metre racing yachts. He told us of his days as an apprentice before the war, and of working on a Dutch coaster bringing Cornish slates from near Penzance to Putney up the Thames. He clearly longed for the open sea and the wind filling his sails, but 'the crew', which was how he referred to his wife, found the rivers and canals more agreeable. Presumably this was because there were more postboxes for her postcard production. 'The crew' wrote on silently, never once referring to an address book, and sticking the stamp on with a flourish when each card was covered in all the legal places. I was reminded by Sabine of a tragic occurrence when, on one of our earlier trips down the Canal du Midi in the South of France, she had written a large number of postcards and had allowed the lot to blow away in a gust of wind. How she had howled as they floated away in the wash of the *Leo*! The cards, together with the Yehudi Menuhin *Teach Yourself Violin*

163

book, had all sunk by the time I had stopped and reversed to recover them.

We slipped down the Neckar, which I am sure is very romantic when it's not cold, damp and grey, as it was that day. We stopped in Mannheim and I went to buy some batteries for our portable radio, bumping into our Rhine pilot who was, of course, carrying his holdall full of dried soup. We set off down the Rhine together and he told us of what had befallen him with the other barges he had taken up to Strasbourg. It seems they'd had a very bad trip with some serious mechanical trouble, and I think he was pleased to be back on board the *Leo* which, with all its failings, always seemed to get you there. We had not far to go on the five-knot current before we turned right at Mainz and into the Main. Sabine and Robert got out their violins and sat at the head of the barge, playing deliciously as we flashed past the village of Nierstein, its beautiful church silhouetted against the world-famous vineyards. The sun shone on Sabine's golden hair and I felt very proud to be her father.

The pilot called up a fuelling barge who came alongside and refuelled us, charging an exorbitant price – probably the highest in Europe – for our diesel. We left the pilot on board the fuelling barge, smoking away just under a huge No Smoking sign. Ray and I had decided to take a chance and go up the Main river without him, as it seemed quite un-necessary and also expensive to have him on board. We had no difficulties at the first couple of locks and moored by a football pitch in Florsheim, a rather pretty place where they made shoes.

I had had an introduction to a very impressive woman by the name of Princess Metternich, and I thought that since she did not live too far away, I would call on her. She lived in a castle on the Rhine, called the Schloss Johannisburg, which was famous for its cellars and excellent white wine. It had been bombed by the Allies during the Second World War – by mistake, unless it was that some pilot wanted to unload his bombs on the way home and thought that it looked a likely target. The old castle had been completely rebuilt, with state help, largely because of its vast wine cellars which had not been too badly damaged by the bombing. The wine there had become famous as a result of a mistake: a messenger, sent by the bishop who owned the estate in the sixteenth century with the message that the grape harvest should begin, was unaccountably delayed for a few days. The result was that the grapes had started to rot on the vine by the time they were gathered, but, surprisingly, tasted delicious. The accident was adopted as a technique, and this is what gives the wine from this vineyard its distinctive bouquet. It is also an example of the discipline of the Germans as a race, for I am sure that neither the French nor the Italians would dream of waiting for orders that would prejudice the harvest, and would have acted on their own accord.

We went over to the castle by car, and the Princess, who is a charming woman, greeted me very cordially. She told me of her days in Berlin during the war, where she and her sister, Russian émigrées, had found work in various government offices. I asked her what it had really been like in those days and, refreshingly, she told me that she and her sister had been pretty girls together and had a fine time of it for the first years, and then, when they had realized the extent of the Nazi barbarism, did what they could with the many languages that they spoke. Her sister had been working for the outstanding Adam von Trott, who many say was the architect of the 20 July plot on Hitler's life. The Princess herself had married a German army officer of the old school and had moved to their estates in Czechoslovakia towards the end of the war, only to find that they had to leave because of the rapid advance of the Russian army. They walked with what they could carry to their other estate: this castle by the Rhine at Schloss Johannisburg.

The Prince was away, so I took the liberty of sitting in the chair that had belonged to *the* Metternich, who was famed for his wiliness at the Congress of Vienna, and had a few irreverent thoughts about world domination. Metternich, according to most of the history books, had been attending a ball in Vienna when the news broke that Napoleon had landed in Cannes, at the start of the campaign that was to end at Waterloo. This unwelcome information had been a real party stopper and the ball had broken up in mid-waltz. The Princess confided that her husband's forebear had actually been in bed at the time, or possibly sitting in the same chair as I was.

The area between the Main and Frankfurt, with Wiesbaden in between, seems like an enormous ribbon development from the road, but from the river it is quite different. The industrial developments, though huge, have somehow been contained and do not seem endless and pointless as they do in Britain or Belgium. One moment there would be an enormous chemical works on the banks of the river, and the next a charming little village set in the midst of trees and fields. I found this very surprising and so we stopped at Höchst, mooring near a boat which was being converted to the height of luxury for taking passengers on all-year-round cruises down the Rhine and into the Low Countries.

The little town was a few hundred yards up the hill through some municipal gardens. Our first task was to fill up with water but surprisingly there were no hydrants about and the nearest tap was in the ladies' toilets in the gardens. The hose just reached, but as I was debating with myself about the right moment to dash in and fix it to the tap, I found myself being eyed very sternly by a German lady. She clearly felt I was up to no good, and, as I was unable to explain why it was necessary to enter the ladies' lavatory and she was clearly not going to make any kind of effort to understand what I had in mind, we were in a stand-off position. She withdrew to gather reinforcements and I sat down on one of the benches

166

and waited till the coast cleared. Eventually the park-keeper arrived, summoned by the informer. I tried to explain what I wanted but, though it was clear that had I had another hundred foot of hosepipe I would have been able to fill up from the gents, he said that it was *ganz verboten* to enter the ladies' toilet under any circumstances, such is the strict adherence to rules in Germany. Who was it that, during the war, called the Germans carnivorous sheep? Defeated, I wound up the hose and returned to the boat. As we had no water Ray and I stayed at the local hotel, which was a huge floating barge, so that we could have a bath before entering Frankfurt.

Our journey had taken on a new aspect. The countryside was no longer familiar and our attempts with the language were extremely basic. Many people that we met spoke English but I was acutely embarrassed by my rudimentary German and wished I had worked harder at it while I was at school. We did not take long to cover the twenty kilometres into Frankfurt but we had no idea where we could moor, which made it a rather nervous trip: unlike Paris, Frankfurt does not have many bridges and along the north bank of the Main there are neat gardens surrounded by trim walls of the regional red sandstone. I decided to stop, in what looked like the city centre, alongside a promenade. I was slightly concerned about the possibility of things getting stolen but I need not have worried. The boat became an instant point of interest and for a couple of hours Ray and I sat talking to passers-by from all over the world. A beautiful girl dressed in the briefest of bikinis went by, draped over the bows of a small speedboat, and greeted us as she passed in a surprisingly low voice. Her 'Hallo boys' turned our heads and our attention from the middle-aged Persian sisters who were telling us about the difficulties they had had in raising money for the poor in Iran from this enormously wealthy city.

It was a holiday weekend and, as luck would have it, I broke a bit off my tooth on some hard German bread and

167

had to have it fixed. There was no possibility of going to a dentist because they had all taken the weekend off, and anyway it is against the rules for good German teeth to break over a weekend. As we approached our mooring, I had noticed that there was an immense hospital on the south bank. I made my way over there and at once became embroiled in the Euro-nightmare of getting free medical care in another European country. It very soon became extremely clear to me that there was no chance of cracking the problem of having no permanent address, and so I asked whether it would be possible to be treated privately. I was told to sit in a huge waiting room, quite empty, in the front row of row upon row of shiny plastic chairs. After some minutes of wondering if this expedition had been a good idea, I heard brisk footsteps approaching. Their owner was a nice Irish girl who had been a dental nurse in Dublin but had not been able to get a job in a hospital here till she spoke German, which she had learned by working in a German butcher's. I liked her at once, and as we walked to the surgery she told me I was in luck as, according to her, the most brilliant young dentist in Germany was going to look after me. The surgery was a gleaming, modern affair and I was told to sit in the chair, where I was left alone. I closed my eyes for a minute and must have dozed off. When I opened them again I found myself looking into the most beautiful pair of clear blue orbs. Their owner turned out to be the brilliant – and beautiful – dentist, who gently fixed my tooth assisted by her Irish handmaiden. I happily paid her, and, for the first time in my life, left a dental surgery walking on air.

Ray decided to fly home to see his family, and I stayed with the boat which meant I could wander about Frankfurt for a few days. Moored up as we were in the equivalent of Hyde Park or Central Park, I had one slight disadvantage – the lack of a hall porter who would have an idea of what was on and what to do. I saw Ray off at the central station on his way to the airport and then, having smartened myself up as best I could, walked into one of Frankfurt's swankiest hotels. It had a large circular lobby and as I paused, uncertain of my direction, I could feel disapproving eyes boring into my baggy blue jeans and unpolished shoes. How could they know that I was one of the few people in the last fifty years who had come from London by water to their hotel lobby? The concierge was a charming Indian which was not what I had expected, and I immediately felt at home. I explained that I wanted to know what was going on in the city and told him how I had arrived. He produced several brochures and a tram timetable and promised to visit the boat on his day off. For a moment I felt tempted to stay in this comfortable hotel and use the hotel telephones instead of having to struggle with the German telephone boxes which are strangely inefficient, but I had a water supply on the quay and I felt it would be abandoning the *Leo* to leave her during the night.

The hotel was near the main station and in the red light district of Frankfurt. The Germans, in public at least, seem to treat sex like some brisk muscular activity which must at all times be efficient – or so the brochures that I had been given would have it. In the streets where I found myself there were many bars which seemed to cater for the ambling American servicemen who roamed the streets in twos and threes. Next there were the brothels which were somehow industrialized, many containing the sexy French word *'amour'* in their names: 'Palais d'Amour' and even 'Sauna d'Amour'. After the *d'amour* group there were a number of establishments which had woven, equally inappropriately, 'Paradise' into their billboards. 'Paradise Garten' was a six-storey building; the girls who were not busy leaning out of the windows and whistling at the crowds were instead trying to catch the eye of some likely chap in the street below.

Near the underground entrance at the top of the Kaiserstrasse, opposite a ribbon of multi-screen porno cinemas, I met some angels – at least if they were not, they were surely blessed with a ticket to heaven. A minibus announcing that it was waging war against AIDS was parked in the middle of the pedestrian zone. There was an orderly queue of heroin addicts waiting to exchange used needles for new ones, a cup of tea and a packet of condoms. I was fascinated by all this, and went to ask the beautiful woman who was running the show with three helpers to tell me about her efforts. She was called Crystal and, curiously, held my hand while we talked, trying to see whether I was genuinely curious or some sort of police spy. She explained that her clients never had any peace from the authorities. In Germany it is against the rules to shoot up 'H', and that meant that you were sent to prison if you were an addict. No attempt was made by the authorities to cure the addicts, and, according to Crystal, there was no use of heroin-substitute drugs to get these poor people off their deadly habit.

Crystal's big breakthrough had happened when she had persuaded the police to give her a hands-off zone ten metres round her little bus, three times a week, so at least the junkies could exchange their needles. She readily admitted that her successes were limited but she told me that she had been pleased when a group of women she had been working with had stopped a man giving a young girl a shot of heroin for the first time. Making people aware of what was right and wrong, and getting them to do something about it themselves, was the only way forward, she said. While we were talking, Crystal's team, Connie, Rosemary and Hubert were dishing out their giveaways, counting the used needles and dispensing the tea. Nothing, absolutely nothing, seemed to shock them more than the police brutality towards these poor wretches – especially in winter. The ways that the addicts had to steal and sell themselves to satisfy their craving were just a way of life, and they had heard all the stories of depravity a thousand times before. In a city where there are 392 different banks, you would think it should be possible to fund an operation like Crystal's, but all she could raise was a small amount from federal funds in Bonn.

When I got back to the boat I found that I had some neighbours from the German yachting fraternity, including the beauty who had hailed me in her bikini with that husky 'Hallo boys'. Her husband was a jolly restaurateur who invited me on board his cabin cruiser for a beer. By the time I had drunk with them and all the other owners of the small flotilla that had moored against the barge, and had returned the compliment with the crate of beer I had bought on our last refuelling stop, a good deal of alcohol had been consumed. One of the owners of the boats, I cannot remember which, had bought a synthesizer but did not know how to work it. The girl in the bikini could play a keyboard and soon became the star of the party, while the men flashed torches over the instructions to turn her perfectly pleasant piano into a large string orchestra. I sat on the deck watching them, and then slipped off to bed, making sure that I had locked myself in as I was sure there would be calls to have yet another nightcap. There were, and I was glad I had battened down the hatches for these hollow-legged hearties were more than a match for me. In the early hours, I heard the boats being untied as they went off to their regular moorings and presumably their normal day's work.

The next day I went by tram to the Leather Museum in Offenbach. The museum was started by a gentleman who got into collecting leather objects early, just after the First World War. He had very little money but managed to assemble, amongst other things, one of the very best collections of genuine North American Indian items including a beautiful pair of beaded moccasins. Since then the collection has grown and houses such diverse items as Napoleon's handbag, as well as a huge range of other things, from Mexican carved leather saddles to the thumbs and sinews of some wretched British officer that a Chinese warlord had cunningly turned into a belt. There were ravishing red leather boots from Hungary and the most delicate ladies' shoes from *fin-de-siècle* Paris. This odd and often eccentric collection demonstrated

171

so great a variety of uses that mankind has made of leather that I thoroughly recommend any who pass nearby to visit it.

On my tramride back to Frankfurt, I sat next to a bright young French student who had a part-time job in the town to learn German and German business methods. She helped me with my inquiries on how to get to Frankfurt Zoo and then very kindly came with me. I have never been fond of zoos but had frequently been told that the zoo in Frankfurt is very splendid. The buildings are extremely efficient and everything was beautifully laid out, but somehow I felt even sorrier for the animals than usual. Now that it is possible to see them in their natural habitat every five minutes on television, I should have thought that the demand for zoos would have dwindled, but I was to discover this did not seem to be the case in Germany.

On the way to the zoo, the French girl prattled on authoritatively about the benefits of the EEC and about how big and efficient everything was going to be, and my heart sank because she really believed it would be the case. How wonderful the Channel Tunnel was going to be, she said, how it was going to bring Europeans together! I remembered the great sense of achievement I had felt when we had successfully made our crossing, and how glad I had been that Britain was an island. I realized that what I was discovering on the journey I was making through the byways of Europe was a million miles away from the economic dreamworld that this girl was telling me about. We arrived at the tram stop outside the zoo and mercifully she had to go and do some more homework for the bright new tomorrow that she and her generation were building.

Ray was returning the following day, so I rose early in the morning to cross the bridge above the boat for a look at the Film Museum on the other side of the river. As I had been sitting on the deck of the barge, thinking about this and that, I had spotted an odd-looking pipe sticking out at right angles from the museum building. I found that on the first floor the museum had constructed a display about the origins of photography, and the pipe that was sticking out was holding the lens for a mock camera obscura, through which I was delighted to be able to see the *Leo* moored on the other side of the Main. The museum cinema was showing their copy of *The Blue Angel* and I spent what my mother would have called a thoroughly sinful morning, watching that marvellous, moving film. I suspect that one of the main reasons that I came into the film business was the sheer bliss of being able to see films in the morning. Now, of course, anyone can see whatever they wish on the television whenever they want, but in my day the idea of even being in a cinema or watching a rehearsal in a theatre before noon sent a tingle of excitement down my spine.

After the film, I had a chat with the librarian of the archive, who told me that there were only two films in their library from the National Socialist era that were still banned. One was virulently anti-Semitic, called, in English, 'Jew Suss' (Jesus), which was blocked for obvious reasons, and the other was a film that the British had banned at the end of the war, about the Boers in South Africa who had found themselves in a British concentration camp at the beginning of the century. My librarian friend felt that the ban should remain, not for political reasons of any sort, but because the film makers had copied the scene from *Battleship Potemkin* where the sailors find weevils in their food. He said that anyone could see these banned films if they wanted to. He was a Berliner and carefully explained to me how only Berlin could have produced Lubitsch and Wilder – probably two of the greatest comedy directors the cinema will ever have. I had to tear myself away from this engaging, witty man, as I could see that Ray had returned and was standing on the deck of the barge on the other side of the river, unable to get in. I had taken the secret key that we kept hidden under the box where the hydraulic controls were kept, as I was afraid that someone had seen me put it away one day.

It was hot and sticky in Frankfurt that August afternoon and Ray was as keen as I was to shake off the smell of the city and press on up the Main to Bamberg and beyond. The Gardner engine on the *Leo* started up with its familiar throaty chug, and we left the last metropolitan city we would pass through till we reached Vienna, which seemed as far away as it did when we had started out, four months before. Ray's weekend at home had only heightened his resolve to see the famed Danube: his stories of our descent of the Rhine had clearly impressed his waterman friends.

CHAPTER ELEVEN
Frankfurt to Nuremberg

Our first few miles out of Frankfurt were uneventful. The River Main wound through carefully controlled green landscapes until we were about ten miles from Aschaffenburg. I had learnt by now that when things were going smoothly with all the *Leo*'s various systems, it was time for caution. I was proved right, for suddenly, in one of the huge locks they have on the Main, Ray shouted to me that there was something wrong. He told me that the engine was running beautifully but that the unimaginable had happened: the propeller had fallen off. This is something that never happens, or at least it should not. We had to get out of the lock as quickly as possible because we were holding up vast Euro-ships waiting to come in.

There were two ways to get the boat out of the lock: one, to drag it manually, the other to take the dinghy off the deck, clamp on the outboard, and push the whole rig from the stern. There was not time for the latter course. Already they were calling in German for us to get out of the lock. So Ray and I got a rope and pulled the wounded *Leo* slowly out of the enormously long lock with all the people in the control tower laughing and pointing at the old-fashioned British way of moving boats on canals. Later, when I explained the very unusual situation in which we found ourselves, they were much more helpful and rang the local diving club who promised to come and dive for the propeller.

We discovered that there was a big harbour at Aschaffenburg, still another two hours away at the speed we were able to push the *Leo* and the barge using the dinghy strapped on the stern. Ray and I took it in turns to steer the dinghy and the *Leo*, and we finally reached the harbour to find to our delight that there was an enormous crane of the most modern variety, used to load blocks of granite from barges on to railway wagons. It was by now late on Friday evening and I did not think there was any chance whatever of getting the *Leo* lifted out of the water before Monday when the office staff of the harbour would be back. On Saturday morning I walked round the harbour and found a huge scrap yard and went into the office and explained my predicament with the aid of drawing and fractured German to the owner, an extremely pleasant man whose daughter lived in England. He told us that he would fix the foreman and get the tug lifted out of the water that morning and put back again on Sunday morning. This was something that would never have happened in England, or indeed anywhere else that I had been to. He also said that he had been cutting up some old British machine tools and we might be in luck and find the 1¾-inch British Standard Fine nut we would require to secure our propeller – if we could find the propeller, that is. We did have a spare propeller but it was one of the ones that I had experimented with earlier and had decided was not big enough.

While the scrapdealer rang the local diving club, who very obligingly arranged with the lock-keepers to dive for our propeller that afternoon, Ray and I pulled out the immensely heavy yellow webbing strops that I had made in London. The crane had the *Leo* out in no time and we soon saw what the trouble was. We had not only lost the propeller and the nut but the key as well. The key is an oblong piece of metal that fits into a slot in the propeller shaft and the propeller itself and stops the propeller twisting off. Now that we knew what we needed, we set out to comb the scrap heaps to try to find a nut that would fit. Eventually we found a heap of old guillotine machines, called 'The Victoria', that had been used to cut up paper. After we located a suitably sized nut

176

the problem was how to get it off. I fetched our blowlamp from the boat and a huge Stillson grip (that is the kind of tool that plumbers are always forgetting). Ray found a long pipe and, while I heated up the rust-and-paint-covered nut with the blowlamp, he put the pipe on the handle of the Stillson and with a huge effort the nut moved free. We hurried back to the boat and tried it on: it fitted – not quite as well as an engineer would have liked, but it fitted. Now we had to get the propeller back.

To our astonishment a smart white Mercedes drew up and a man stepped out dressed in a German huntsman costume complete with hat and feather. It was our scrap merchant friend who was off to his domain, since it was Saturday afternoon, to try his hand at a bit of sport, which I suppose meant shooting anything that was in season. The lock where we had lost the propeller was on his way and he wanted to have a word with the diving club to be sure that everything was in order. The frogmen were ready, Ray told them where he thought the propeller would be, and the lock was emptied so the divers would not have to dive so deep. The constant flow of shipping was diverted through the parallel lock. Almost at once the first diver flipped over backwards into the murky water and after about two minutes came up with our propeller. We could not believe our luck and gave the divers a suitable present for their club.

We hired a cab back to the harbour and the boat, and, as soon as we arrived, a very cross gentleman turned up asking who had given us permission to have our boat there as it was against all the rules for a private boat to be repaired in the grounds of a state-controlled enterprise. Fortunately there are sensible people in every country, so I pointed to the very tough-looking foreman on the other side of the dock who was directing the movement of a large granite block and told my inquisitor that he was the one to quiz. As if by magic the man's temper cooled and he became extremely civil and wished us luck on our journey. I suppose the burden of those

177

German rules had suddenly been lifted from his shoulders now that he knew someone else was responsible.

We made a new key for the shaft, put the propeller back and jammed on the nut. I would have liked to have drilled through the shaft and put a pin through it and the nut so the nut could not work its way off again, but we had no electrical supply to run our drill. Ray painted below the waterline with a special anti-rust paint we had brought from London and the *Leo* was ready to be lifted back into the water at seven the next morning.

After the slag heaps of the harbour at Aschaffenburg the countryside was extremely beautiful. We pushed on along the Main valley through Würzburg where I had decided we should not stop as we were getting very behind schedule. I greatly regretted the decision because the town looked extremely interesting. On the outskirts there were a number of tented camps for holidaymakers which were clearly very popular but it was concentrated camping of a type that only the Germans seem to enjoy. I remember once having witnessed a startling example of this concentrated camping, when I had been staying the night on a recce for a film I was producing in Egypt, called *Death on the Nile*, at Abu Simbel, in a dilapidated rest house. Most of the tourists who go there fly in for the day and are flown out again after they have seen the amazing statues which were moved up the mountain when the Russians flooded the Nubian Valley to create the Aswan Dam. To my surprise a strange-looking bus had arrived full of Germans who had travelled across a great deal of desert from Tripoli in this vehicle, called a Rotel, in which up to twenty people sleep in what can only be described as filing-cabinet drawers. They seemed to love their journey though, and built a campfire in the grounds of the rest house and sang German camping songs far into the clear desert night under a canopy of stars.

That night we stopped in a remote village, with a pretty church, called Lohr, situated on the banks of the Main. The evening was remarkable as it seemed to be the night when a certain larva hatched and a host of insects sprang from the river for a night of violent love only to die the next morning. It was dark by half past eight and an hour later the barge was covered in an inch of white-winged insects with yellow bodies. There were so many that I had to sweep them off the deck and into the river in huge piles. I suppose it was the lights on the boat that attracted them to the *Leo* but I must say I was awed by this natural manifestation of energy and waste. I can still hear the frantic whirring of their wings as they feverishly copulated for the first and last time.

The next day started uneventfully enough. There was a green and white helicopter patrolling up and down the river and we waved cheerfully back at it as it passed overhead – but we were in for an unpleasant shock. Soon after three in the afternoon, a large, fast, mean-looking patrol launch came briskly alongside. A tall German river policeman with film-star good looks and a heavy gun on his hip stepped on board and demanded to see our papers. We produced the papers, which were in order, and Ray presented not only his Waterman's Licence for the Thames but also his apprenticeship indentures. The apprenticeship system is still operated on the Thames: when a boy is taken on by a master the apprenticeship document is ceremoniously cut in half. When the boy has served his time he gets his master's half back. Sadly none of these proofs of experience – as if any were needed after travelling so far – were of any interest to the river policeman. He insisted that we stop at the next lock and consider that we were under barge arrest till we had cleared our position and taken on a pilot.

As he left, he told us that we could eat rather well in a little pub in the neighbouring village. The events of the day had done nothing to cheer me up so I decided that we should leave the boat, tied up as she was at Wipfeld lock, and have

179

a hot meal and some beer. We walked through the fields and came upon this very unpromising little village that had no signs whatsoever to make the traveller welcome. Eventually we found an open door and went inside to a small bar where we sat down. Two enormous people came out of the little kitchen and asked us almost in unison what we should like to eat. I said we did not mind. They went away and within ten minutes the wife started to lay out the most sumptuous spread before us. Local beer, so dark that you could not see through it when you held it up to the light, red cabbage, bits of meat, herring, cream – within half an hour our situation with the police did not seem so bad and soon it became quite funny. If we had to be arrested, then it was good news that we were near this hostelry. More and more delicious things were put before us and I began to wonder whether a pretty innkeeper's daughter would suddenly appear, but I suspect that my hosts had probably been too busy cooking and eating for much to have sprung from their loins.

At eight the next morning, a round-faced, jolly man arrived and made us understand that he was to be our pilot. 'What about the *Polizei*?' I inquired, and he made it plain that all would be well and all was fixed. I arranged a rate with him and we set sail through the lock that had barred our way the night before. I wondered what had happened with the police but all seemed to be well and all the barges we passed seemed to know our pilot, who was called Gerhard. It turned out that he was the local icebreaker captain and he was usually free in the summer for pilotage up and down the Main. He told us that only certain sections of the Main froze because of the huge amount of warm water that was pumped into the river from the outputs of the nuclear plants. I found it unnerving to think that so much hot water was pumped into the river and I wondered what else was – and yet the Germans are renowned for being extremely good at keeping their rivers clean. After a couple of hours the police boat arrived again and the young officer explained that he had gone to a lot of trouble to ring the authorities in Bonn and had got them to admit that the papers we had left some doubt about whether or not we should have had a pilot on the Main. He had been able to persuade them that we should not be fined, which in the normal way we would have been; at the same time he managed to indicate how much his helmsman loved Scotch whisky. We said goodbye and as they sped off I threw a plastic bottle of Scotch into the cabin to see how quick their reactions would be, and was amused to see they failed to catch it. They waved their thanks when they found the bottle had not broken.

Gerhard had been around a bit and he had some amusing stories to tell about the life he led, which was very similar to that of watermen everywhere. He told us how one of the best contracts on the river was bringing American coal which was shipped from the States to Rotterdam and then brought all the way up the Rhine and then the Main to the American service bases round Bamberg. What it must cost the Americans to do this is unthinkable, but it kept American miners in work and the barges running. The only problem in this little scheme, in which somebody somewhere must surely be making money for themselves, was that the coal was of a kind that the Green Party in Germany said was polluting their atmosphere.

Gerhard knew that there was a four-day beer festival in Bamberg which was starting that night, so he got off at the next lock and phoned his friend Fritz to find us somewhere to moor the boat in the centre of Bamberg, a mooring which could only be reached by a private lock which only Fritz, who ran the local pleasure boats, could open. We arrived at the lock, which was only just large enough for us to get through, where Fritz and his wife and sons were all waiting for us. They were all licensed pleasure-boat skippers and they completely controlled all the boats in Bamberg and were doing very well on it. Fritz took over the wheel for the last tricky kilometre into Bamberg.

181

The town was dressed over all, as it were, for its festival. The gaily striped marquees and the coloured lights were very pretty against the old houses lining the river. Fritz brought us into a mooring close to his boats and next to the public lavatories which, as the lady who ran them wistfully remarked, were at their busiest during beer festivals. As we tied up, a huge tray of glasses, each with over two inches of brandy, was produced to welcome us. A reporter from Radio Bamberg leapt on board and said how happy they all were that a British boat had come all the way from London to be there for their festival. It seemed churlish to contradict him. It was one of the most curious things about our trip, that people were most interested to find out why we had come to a place, not where we had been or where we were going. But it's a bit like that with holiday snaps. Nobody cares where you've been unless they've been there themselves.

We stayed in this beautiful old city for a couple of days. The festival was mostly populated with out-of-towners who had come to drink gallons of beer and feast off the hundreds of ducks that were turning on spits outside most of the restaurants. Bands played German marches, people sang and swayed to the music. I could almost smell the heartiness amongst the sauerkraut and roasting ducks. A team of Italians was making pizzas in a booth and proudly told me that they had composed a song specially for the occasion. The problem with their masterpiece was that its lyric consisted of only one word, 'Pizza', repeated over and over again.

Later, I talked to a monk who ran weekends up at his monastery on the top of the hill for people in need of silence. He was an amusing man and I am sure that his courses must have been spiritually very refreshing. His order, founded in the twelfth century, was not allowed to possess any animal larger than an ass and as we walked past the monastery's garage, he said that their order had rationalized this to owning nothing bigger than a Volkswagen. Mercedes were out.

Bamberg was where the old Ludwig Canal ended with lock number 100. Charlemagne had dreamed of a canal linking the Main to the Danube, thus linking the North Sea to the Black Sea. He had tried to join the two rivers but had failed just before the project had reached the Danube. Ludwig had succeeded and the canal had remained in use up to the middle of the Second World War when the Allies had bombed it because they had had information that submarine parts were being moved along it. Virtually all the canal has now disappeared, except for the last lock which has been preserved in Bamberg, and which has a beautiful lock-keeper's house. These houses were standard all along the canal, apparently, and had been designed by Ludwig's personal architect. The ancient gentleman who was the present incumbent was quite small but extremely enthusiastic. He nearly came to grief when he demonstrated to me how the footbridge mechanism worked by winding a handle: it caught him unawares and the weight of the gate caused him to be lifted helplessly into the air on the end of the handle.

The festival was still going on when we made a rather perilous descent of the River Regnitz with the tide under us. The river flows fast and there was not room for us to turn, which meant that when we approached Fritz's lock on the way out we had to throw a line to one of Fritz's sons who quickly put the eye over a bollard so that we could check our far too rapid descent – going full astern was no use at all.

From Bamberg, we joined the uncompleted Rhine–Main– Donau Canal as far as Nuremberg, a hard day's run through a huge canal with very little traffic on it. We reached the end of the canal at sunset with an unreasonable sense of disappointment that, after all these hundreds of waterborne miles, the two vessels would have the indignity of being loaded on a lorry and driven down a motorway to the Danube. Of course, we'd known all along that the canal

183

wouldn't be open officially, but sometimes you find routes open before the officially designated day.

I had, of course, anticipated that we would need some pretty heavy lifting gear to get the barge out of the water and had spoken to a few crane-hire firms before making a final choice. Almost as soon as we arrived at the dockside a tall melancholy man from the crane firm appeared and quickly summed up the situation which for him was a mere bagatelle, he said. There was something about his melancholy that made me believe that he probably knew what he was talking about and I trusted him at once. He had made arrangements with the port authorities in Nuremberg to lift our craft out on to their special reinforced dock in three days' time. He planned to use two cranes, each with a capacity of 150 tons. Cranes are rated for lifting weights straight up: as soon as the crane arm jibs out, the amount that they can lift is rapidly reduced and since these cranes were going to have to lean out, as it were, to pick up the barge, it was necessary to have a considerable over-capacity. The only problem that he foresaw was the police who would not let us travel during the day down the motorway, which made me think in Wagnerian terms of our huge barge careering through the night towards Regensburg and the Danube.

Nuremberg, once described as the 'jewel of the Third Reich', is a very Bavarian town. There are a great number of American servicemen in camps round the city, I suppose because of its proximity to Czechoslovakia. I wandered round the town, not finding it very sympathetic, and became an- noyed by the brass ring in the marketplace, which, according to legend, had been miraculously placed by some brilliant apprentice round a cast-iron upright, part of the decorative fence surrounding the cross in the marketplace: apparently he had achieved this without a join in the ring. The tourists love it of course and fondle the seamless brass ring in the hope that it will bring them luck. If they were to run their fingers, as I did, up the back of the cast iron that held the ring, they would find the cast iron had been joined together after the ring had been put on.

I strolled round to the harbour master's office and was invited to visit the works at the end of the canal where they were putting the finishing touches to one of the vast locks. I climbed down into the lock which was completely empty and found myself one hundred feet below the top. At one end of the lock were a number of small furry bodies spreadeagled on the floor. They were voles which had probably been making their journey along their accustomed routes and had fallen into this vast hole by mistake and perished.

This vast project, linking the North Sea to the Black Sea, through linking the Rhine to the Danube, has been under construction for many years and is now due to open in 1992. The political problems that made the Germans fear that the Eastern Bloc countries would dominate the freight rates of Europe if they let them pass through the canal and their country have largely disappeared, and the opposition of the Green parties has been to some extent silenced, so perhaps this time a project might open when the authorities say it will. The canal requires a vast amount of high-level water to replenish it when the huge locks are opened and shut and so two immense artificial lakes have been created on an arid plateau nearby. This source of water is sufficent to generate enough electrical power not only to pay for the running of the canal but over the years it will also pay for a large part of the construction cost of the canal. Each time the locks are opened only 40 per cent of the water is lost to the next level: the remaining 60 per cent is pumped into huge holding tanks ready for the next ship to pass through.

I was pleased to learn from the people showing me round that the Green Party had forced them to make some concessions for having driven this vast scar through one of the most beautiful parts of Europe. They showed me some ponds beside the canal which they said were resting places for ducks. To my untrained eye they looked just like lay-bys on main roads. I suppose that in fifty years' time, when the countryside has healed up a bit, this method of moving huge quantities of heavy merchandise will be a great deal better for the environment than moving it by road or rail, but at the moment it is a matter of faith to be able to visualize the finished product.

All the earth-moving equipment used in the construction work is enormous, and on the sector they were excavating when I was there they had built a substantial hill about half a mile from the canal: so substantial that the day after my visit, there was a heavy rainfall and thirty million cubic metres of mud and stones slipped like a vast lake of custard into the valley below. The sides of the canal were made with stones and nuggets of concrete over which was sprayed liquid concrete. On top of that were placed wire netting and more liquid concrete. The final stage was large aggregate and asphalt placed on the sloping sides. Imagine how it annoyed the construction company to have to stop and make a dent in this orderly progress to construct a lay-by for ducks.

The day came for the lift and we took the boats from where we had moored to their appointed place – only to find it occupied by a German barge which had to load a cargo of nuclear-reactor parts which had been brought by heavy lorry from Austria, and were to be shipped to Rotterdam by barge and then to who knew where. The skipper explained that there was a problem: one of the bridges under construction that we had passed under near Würzburg had collapsed, killing a number of workmen, and the river was closed to all traffic until further notice. No one knew how long that might be. His contract was only for delivery of the goods so if he could not get through he would lose the work, which had naturally made him rather glum. The cranes and the heavy lorries were assembling and very soon there was a large group of people trying to sort things out. The drivers of the heavy lorries from Austria wanted to go home but could not because they could not unload their crates. The two lorries that had come to carry the boats off could not be loaded because the German barge was in the place where the cranes had been set up. Finally a small red car arrived full of fairly disreputable men who appeared to be the agents for the nuclear parts and told the barge to move while we were loaded.

I must say that I was extremely anxious when the barge was lifted out of the water because the stitching of the yellow strops began to pop in an alarming manner, but the melancholy crane manager and his calm, gum-chewing crane-drivers took no notice. With infinite care they lifted the old girl out of the water and jibbed their cranes round in perfect unison until they had the barge directly over the waiting lorry. Once the barge had been correctly positioned on the lorry and the amount of overhang had been carefully measured, the vehicle was moved out of the way to make room for the other one which would carry the *Leo*. When both vehicles were loaded, the mournful man explained that we had a problem because we were above the regulation height for the police permissions that he had obtained. I never got to the bottom of why this had happened but in any case it meant that we had to take down the entire crane arm on the barge, and cut down our blue flag board as well as a number of other bits such as the handrail between the two boats. The lorry drivers were most sympathetic, realizing that we were in the grip of a bureaucratic muddle, and soon cut off the offending bits that could not be dismantled.

My main preoccupation once the problem of the height had been solved was unblocking the outside of the sewage-tank drain which had got firmly blocked by earth, and other more unpleasant substances, when we ran aground from time to time. Now the *Leo* was out of the water I had an opportunity to tackle the problem. Through fatigue or sheer stupidity I was of course standing under the drain when it finally disgorged itself, much to the amusement of the drivers.

187

As I paid the mournful man the £4500 this lift was costing, he told me a story which perhaps accounted for his perpetual gloom. He told me that he had only once been to London, to sell a very large nineteenth-century French painting owned by his family, at one of the leading London auction rooms. When he had arrived, he took the painting to the auction rooms to be told by the expert for that type of painting, a certain Anthony Blunt, that it was a fake. Blunt added that he had just sold the original to a client in America. A few days later, after having seen the sights of London, the mournful man went back to the auctioneers to collect the painting, but it had mysteriously disappeared. The auctioneers were eager to pay out the insurance money, which was only a fraction of what the painting was worth, he said, for he had no doubt that his was the original. He left in a fury and later accepted the insurance money feeling the British had done him down.

The police, for whom we were waiting to inspect the load, arrived just as the sun was setting. The bargeman who had been held up by the collapsed bridge had, by now, loaded his huge boxes of nuclear spares and was waiting for news of the repairs to the bridge. Suddenly all the measurements were done and the convoy set sail, as it were, down the motorway with Ray driving the 2CV while I drove a hired car with a huge flashing sign, fixed by magnets to the roof, to warn people that a very heavy convoy was on the move.

CHAPTER TWELVE

Nuremberg to Passau

It took us about five hours to cover the hundred or so kilometres to Regensburg, the furthest point north on the Danube. When we woke in the morning we found ourselves on the side of a dock full of barges from the Eastern Bloc countries. The East had really begun. I watched a Rumanian bargeman feeding his chickens that he kept in a hutch on the deck. The Germans said they kept livestock on board because they could not afford the price of German food but it may have been because they liked fresh eggs. The Germans seem to resent the way the Rumanian government has put a price of £12,000 on anyone of German origin who wishes to leave Rumania. So, if you had a German mother-in-law in Rumania, you'd have to decide whether £12,000 was worth it!

The lorry drivers were very keen to put the old *Leo* back together again in just the state they found her and managed to persuade the dock engineers to lend us their welding gear. By breakfast time all was back as it should have been and a fresh coat of paint had been brushed over the black weld marks. We then went round to the works canteen in the docks, a splendid place with jolly waitresses, whom the lorry drivers chatted up and who produced an extremely filling goulash soup with frankfurters, a dish which seemed to span the ethnic frontiers. Once the gang had breakfasted, the unloading began and the operation went with typical German efficiency: suddenly we were actually floating on the Danube.

The first person from the world of Regensburg to visit us was a Hungarian: Hungarians are nearly always first when someone new and potentially interesting turns up in town. The young man who arrived had been educated at Harrow and consequently spoke perfect English. He had been sent by his boss, Captain Ott, who arrived soon afterwards with instructions on how to complete our papers to proceed down the Danube. He told me that Regensburg had been one of the centres of the salt route when salt was brought from the Far East; the caravans crossed the bridge that had stood in Regensburg for centuries.

Captain Ott was one of the many men that I was to meet who had worked on the Danube all his life, and was a true romantic. He had literally run away to sea when his father, also a Danube captain, had forbade him to. He had become the youngest captain in service anywhere on the Danube and had many a story to tell of a certain Captain Frolich with whom he had worked as mate and who was later to be our pilot. He told of derring-do, of manoeuvring a vast bridge into position with a series of barges and tugs, and the delights of his favourite haunts which I suspect only the Danube sailors know of. Captain Ott had been offered a job in the front office of the shipping company he worked for because of his expertise in knowing just how far a barge could be loaded at any season. This required a very expert knowledge of the water levels up and down the Danube and the length of the voyage. If the barge was overloaded and he knew that two days before it had rained heavily in the mountains he could gauge whether there was a chance that the cargo would get through with the draught it had or whether it would have to be unloaded into smaller craft.

The trade on the Danube was very much controlled by the Soviets, who manned their craft with service personnel so there was no question of having to make a profit in commercial terms. The Soviets were the main suppliers of coal and coke to the great Austrian steel works at Linz. If the Austrians ever fell out with their big Russian brothers they would have a thin time of it indeed. Most of the barges that came up the

Danube from the east were without motors and therefore had to be towed by huge tugs that varied enormously in age, but, however old, were still capable of making considerable headway over an eighteen-kilometre current with a string of 3000-ton barges behind them. Because of the length of the tows it was necessary for the barges to be manned and to be steered all the time they were under way, so that the tow could negotiate corners successfully.

It was a bit like the boyhood of Raleigh as Ray and I sat and listened to Captain Ott talking about his life on the Danube. He told us of how, when he had decided on the advice of his wife to take the job in the office, he had hidden his car behind a tree to watch his beloved ship steam off down the Danube for the first time without him in charge, and had shed a tear or two. I do not believe that any modern woman can ever understand the romance that a boat has for a man. How can they? Men do not understand it themselves, but there is something there which most women fear and distrust; they fear the seductress over whom they have no control who gently rocks their men to sleep at night and leads them into distant temptations and out from under their thumbs.

In order for us to leave the harbour, Captain Ott had arranged for an enormous man, the skipper of a barge from the company that Ott worked for, to pilot us the ten kilometres to the centre of Regensburg, which I thought was hardly necessary. I was wrong, for the current was extremely strong and we made very little headway: it took us a full two hours to get up to a berth next to a Rumanian tug that was waiting for its barges to be unloaded before taking them back to that sad benighted country.

We tied up and Ray went back to the harbour to collect our little car so that we could load it on board the next day before the pilot arrived. It was clear to me that the journey to Vienna was going to be very swift indeed and there would be no sense in leaving the car behind and coming back to collect it

191

later. I went to chat to the crew on the Rumanian tug, taking them a pack of cigarettes which I swapped for some eggs from their marine hencoop. Later, the captain, an incredibly thin man in a well-worn suit which he had clearly just taken from storage, came on board the *Leo* with a bottle of Rumanian-type champagne. He welcomed us very charmingly to the Danube, expressing the hope that we would have many wonderful memories, and then began to tell us of his life on the boats. Rumanians who are permitted to travel outside their country are rare indeed and these boat people are among the privileged few. We did not speak of politics at all, but, after he left, having told us where his favourite mooring places were, I noticed that when he got back to his tug he was grilled by one of the crew. I wondered which one of them was the secret service man. I am afraid I am naive enough not to care and tend to take people as I find them.

Ray had parked our car next to a fine fifteenth-century salt storehouse, about fifty yards from where we had moored. After all the excitement of our first day on the Danube, I, at least, was dead to the world but woke at dawn to find that the *Leo* seemed to be in the midst of a crowd. I pulled on an anorak and went up on deck to find the most astonishing scene of devastation. The salt storehouse, after surviving five hundred years of war, plague and pestilence, had burned down during the night, leaving vast smouldering timbers pointing like great black fingers to the sky. People stood around in the cold morning light looking stunned, while the fire brigade and the police cordoned everything off. I woke Ray, who had also managed to sleep through the whole event, and asked him exactly where he had left the car.

He pointed, somewhat mournfully, at a huge heap of smoking debris that a bulldozer was pushing together. I went to inquire where our car might be and found a policeman who said that they had towed away a couple of wrecks to the police pound at the back of the police station. When I went round there, I found that the car was a complete wreck, and quite happily signed the papers for its official burial by the appropriate department.

Regensburg was a town that I found myself really at home in. Down on the quayside by the rushing Danube stream, there was a sausage kitchen, run by a lady who had been cooking her sausages there since the last year of World War One. This meant she had been turning over bangers on her griddle for seventy years and remarkably fine she looked on it. I soon discovered there was a kind of sausage dynasty in Regensburg, for her niece – and incidentally her heir – had married an ex-heavy-lorry salesman who had brilliantly expanded the sausage empire into a chain of shops and regular restaurants. The delicious sausages that had become so famous were made, apparently, solely from shin of pork, and for true perfection should be eaten with some of the eighty tons of sauerkraut the enterprise produced every year. One night when the sausage czar was in his cups, he hinted that there had been rumours that the fire which had burnt down the salt house had been started deliberately. After five hundred years of standing in the same place and burning down on the night we arrived, I think he probably had a point.

In the town hall, the guidebook told me that they had the last original torture chamber in Germany here in this odd and enduring town. They had called it a 'questioning room' when it had been in full swing some centuries before. If you were accused you were questioned with the help of a number of devilish devices for stretching your arms or cracking your spine. If, under pressure, you confessed, you were dragged before a people's court where you had a chance to deny the charges, but the catch was that if you did that, the whole process started all over again. This happened three times in all and if you were still alive at the end of it and still denied the charges, you were allowed to go free.

The town is rich because it has a number of high-tech industries that have moved to the area, such as Siemens and BMW – the latter has one of the most modern car plants in

Europe. Ray was an enthusiast for BMWs so we went out to have a guided tour of the plant kindly arranged by the sausage czar. The guide who showed us round this glistening plant kept saying that only two years before the meadows where this factory had been built had been full of sheep. I felt the sheep probably had hornrimmed glasses and read the *Financial Times* in the German edition. The plant is run on the modern system whereby everything that it does not produce itself comes in from local factories at the very last minute – and these factories' output is controlled by the computer at the main plant. I was curious to know what would happen if there was a strike in one of the subsidiary plants and I was assured that there were no strikes in Germany, at least not here.

We walked from one huge shed to the next and watched fascinated as these symbols of modern life were rapidly assembled in a myriad shapes and colours. It is possible to order one of about three hundred different types of wing mirror, or so it seemed. When I mischievously tried to put one of the robots off its singular course by walking very closely in front of its guidance sensors as it transported a fully finished car to the inspection bay, I was briskly told not to provoke it as if it were a sleeping dog! As I walked out of the last stage of this dream factory, it occurred to me that these people were making the dreams that the old studios in Hollywood used to supply with the great films of the thirties and forties.

Far away, on the hills on the other side of the Danube from the factory, stood glistening in the sun the Temple of Valhalla, Ludwig's tribute to the minds of the great men that had made Germany famous a century before. This great Grecian classical structure stood on the top of a small hill overlooking the river. The Germans have resisted spoiling its natural outline by refusing to place railings round the gigantic stone stages, in spite of the protests from the relatives of the Japanese tourists, who, while taking snaps of the magnificent columns, had taken that one step further back than they should have done and plunged thirty feet to the next level of unpardoning granite.

As I walked back to the boat that evening, I mused on the Germany I was discovering. The technical pursuit of perfection was obvious at every turn. The BMW plant made what everyone has come to believe is a very superior car, but will it be remembered in five hundred years' time? The Temple of Valhalla with its marble busts of Beethoven and Schiller seemed to me to reflect virtues more durable than any technical achievement. As I walked past the docks, I saw the shaded red lights of the Palais d'Amour which was clearly part of the same chain as the ones in Frankfurt, with its neat window boxes full of red geraniums, and a discreet pornographic video flickering half-hidden in the doorway to welcome the punter as he mounts the steps for his ration of heaven or, in this case, *Himmel*. I remembered at the tender age of thirteen lying in bed at my boarding school listening to my dormitory prefect reading a chapter from Smollett which ended, 'And so, dear reader, I shall not burden you with the mystery of hymen.' I burned to be burdened and when I was, finally, I found out it was a great deal more mysterious than I had ever imagined.

Ray and I took the *Leo* for a day out up the Danube without the barge, travelling as far as the gorges at Kelheim and past the place where the new Rhine–Main–Donau Canal will join the Danube. The gorges are very impressive and I watched a climber scale the vertical cliffs above the raging river as we plugged away to reach the top of the gorge. We picnicked and chatted about our adventures so far and fell to wondering what our new pilot, Captain Frolich, was going to be like. Because of the great distances that we would inevitably travel due to the speed of the river, the new pilot would have to come prepared to stay on board at night because there was very little chance of him being in a position where he could take the train home at night. So it was with some trepidation that we returned down the rushing Danube to Regensburg. It was on that trip that I calculated that the *Leo* travelled faster than she had ever done before (if you do not count the motorway), at the dizzying speed of 22 kilometres per hour.

I had decided that as we were now going off into the real distance we should have a short-wave radio so that we could call London, or rather, Portishead Radio, direct. While it had been possible to get to a telephone without too much difficulty thus far on our journey, the great distances between towns and the remoteness of some of the reaches of the Danube made a short-wave radio advisable. The two young men who came to fix it were extremely efficient and did the job quickly without any fuss. The curious thing about it was that although they were able to do all the tests and get it functioning, they did not know how to call anyone up because a licence was needed for that. I had a licence but I had to spend some hours reading the instructions in German before I heard the welcoming voice at the other end at Portishead Radio asking my ship's name (Lima-Echo-Oscar-November-Tango-Yankee-November-Echo) with a pronounced West Country burr.

Regensburg has been a crossroads for travellers for centuries because the bridge used to be the only one across the Danube for miles on either side. Tucked away in a little back street was a Czech bookseller who, on hearing my British accent, told me his life story, which should have been on the shelves with the fiction. He had been in the diplomatic service at the beginning of the war and then had joined the British special forces and had been dropped into France, where he seems to have spent the war. He was returned to England and soon after decided to go back to Czechoslovakia to see his family. At Calais he was kidnapped by the Czech secret service and returned home under arrest where he was sentenced to twelve years' hard labour in a quarry. After two years of this he escaped and returned to Germany where he lived in a refugee camp for ten years. During this time he worked at the library in Munich which gave him a great knowledge of books. The British authorities were due to pay him a pension but it took a decade and a half for him to establish his identity and claim his money. Now he is rich and one of the leading experts, or so he claims, on German-language books in Turkey. I realized that, now that we were over the European watershed which lies between Nuremberg and Regensburg, I should be hearing a lot of tales embroidered with oriental splendour like this. But then perhaps it was the truth.

Captain Frolich, our pilot, was due to join us the next day from Linz where he lived, which was downstream about two hundred miles, in Austria. His friend Captain Ott had invited Ray and me to have dinner with him and his wife Christine at their house in a little village just outside Regensburg. We took a taxi and found them in the garden of a house that he and Christine had built with their own hands. The meal was very memorable because their next-door neighbours were Catalans and had come over to cook the most magnificent paella I have ever tasted. This kindness, and many others that we had found in Regensburg, convinced me that it is a very special city, one that has long had a spirit of independence which I hope it never loses.

At seven thirty the next day, Captain Frolich arrived with his Burberry neatly folded over his arm. He was a huge, neat man who spoke no English at all except for one mixed-language phrase that served for many occasions which was, '100 per cent *Absolut Catastroph*' which covered anything from my bad mooring techniques to Ray not stirring his goulash properly, but it was always said with great good humour and we soon grew very fond of him. He was a superb boat-handler and swung the *Leo* neatly in the current as we headed downstream out of Regensburg and down the Danube, passing right under the portals of Valhalla.

Our first stop was at a town called Straubing which lay at kilometre 2222 from the mouth of this enormous river. The kilometres on the Danube are marked with large white boards displaying the number of the kilometre. Every hundred metres is a smaller board, with the half kilometre marked by a plus sign. This way of marking is extremely easy to read and a great deal easier than the official Danube charts. These are like no other charts that I have seen in that they have a complicated system of folded paper, so that when the river bends the chart is folded to bend also, representing the course of the river. When I pulled out my copy to show the Captain he laughed and indicated that the only time that professional Danube men ever used those was when there had been an accident, to establish their alibi.

One of the great problems we were to face on the river was a lack of suitable places to moor. The sides are rocky and the current swift, and the alternatives are either anchoring – which is fine if the river is wide enough – or finding a pontoon which won't have one of the frequent passenger boats arriving while you are tied up. Straubing had such a pontoon and we made our touch. At the end of the gangway was a small municipal garden which had been turned into a permanent exhibition for the local sculptors who, to my eye at least, were a talentless lot, as were a group of artists we had met in Regensburg who seemed to do their best business by shocking their would-be clients with lurid pornographic paintings and then selling them something far more modest to assuage the guilt they had been made to feel for not having the guts to hang a depiction of a six-foot phallus in their drawing room.

The Captain then revealed one of his great talents. He had brought a parcel of food with him and during the day he had been preparing a goulash for his first night aboard. Very much on our best behaviour, Ray and I laid the table and sat down while this vast man doled out, with incredibly neat movements, beautifully cooked rice which he had cooked with lemon – plus his delicious red goulash. He had, he said, made enough to last us a couple of days and when he saw

Bamberg, unscathed by modernity.

The town hall, Bamberg.

Into the Danube at last, Regensburg.

Inset, the *Leo* keeps the red duster flying on the motorway.

Captain Frolich making do on the Danube.

The blue Danube, Melk.

how successful he had been promised to make us 'Matrosen Fleisch' next, which he said meant 'sailor's meat' and was a mixture of beef and anchovies: Ray looked a little doubtful but I liked the sound of it.

Our next stop was to visit my daughter's former German mistress who had come to teach in a boys' school in Metten. She was a brisk German girl who had tried very hard to get to understand the British by taking enormous walks round London and the suburbs. Her view of life in London was very refreshing and I had always enjoyed her swift prattle and slight accent. The school she worked in was a fine old school run by monks, who had been recently forced to take in girls. She proudly showed us the library built by the Aram brothers, a fine pair of architects in the eighteenth century. The library had a very interesting cataloguing system which consisted of paintings on the ceiling of the type of books that you were likely to find in the section underneath. For example, if you wanted to find a book on astronomy, you'd look for the picture of the moon and stars. She came to see us off at the landing stage and waved a red silk handkerchief as we slipped away down the river – for some reason I felt homesick at that moment.

An hour later, we had arrived in Passau and tied up in the middle of the old town where three rivers, the Ilz, the Danube and the Inn meet. Up until the point on the Danube where the Inn meets it, the Inn produces much more water than the Danube and so, by sheer volume of water, the Danube should really be called the Inn. Passau is a fine old town, but on the day we arrived it was clear that something unusual was happening. There were a number of coaches which must have brought a large number of people into the town. I inquired what was going on and was told that the Neo-Nazi Party of Passau had been allowed to hire the town's official assembly rooms for a meeting. Ever curious, I walked up the hill to have a look and found that there was quite a large crowd, composed mostly of policemen, standing in front of the hall. Inside, the Neo-Nazis were having their meeting, and standing about in the street were the opposition, mostly from the German Green Party who looked very much like the demonstrators who had been campaigning for nuclear disarmament in the 1960s.

I asked a number of people what it was all about, and it transpired that in Passau there are very serious unemployment problems and the Neo-Nazis were spouting the same old fascist slogans about 'foreigners out' that the world had heard in the 1930s. So many Turks have been brought in to do the menial tasks over the past few decades that now that the economy has contracted a bit, it is the poor native German-born workers who are out of work – or so the neo-Nazis say. I watched the crowds surround the Nazis as they left the hall and barrack them as they walked to their buses through a phalanx of police efficiently clad in the most modern types of riot gear. Apart from a few hurled insults nothing happened – except that just about everybody who had been at the demonstration was filmed by a police video unit, using telescopic lenses on a number of cameras dotted round the neighbouring buildings. I felt rather odd now that I was on the official German police files as a demonstrator.

During the demonstration, I met a gentleman in a beret with a very dirty collar who asked me to come and visit him in his house nearby in the woods. I went to see him and found a veritable Dr Dolittle, completely surrounded by animals which all roamed around in and out of his house, a wooden shack perched on the side of a wooded hill. He explained to me that after his wife had died he had given up regular contact with human beings because he found that animals were far more romantic. He told me that the goose, Anton, was the night watchman and was very fond of his kitten. The lamb and the poodle were the best of friends and all of them got on with Lisa the donkey. The African parrot seemed to care only for him and was perched on his shoulder – hence the soiled collar. He lived a strange life but his passion for the animals was intense and they responded with affection. He told me he had been wounded at the Battle of Stalingrad but had managed somehow to survive. I suppose it was little wonder that after such a war he was particularly interested in seeing that Fascism was not allowed to rear its ugly head again, hence his attendance at the demonstration.

Passau Cathedral has the world's largest organ, or so the guidebook would have it. This great machine is extremely beautiful and has 17,000 pipes which make the most magnificent sound. It is one of the most popular attractions in Passau for the tourists who queue up for hours in the cathedral square waiting for the doors to open for the daily concert at noon. I talked to one of the organists who clearly did not approve of the vast numbers of visitors coming to the cathedral and had some very uncharitable things to say about these hordes of people. Musically the organ sounds quite superb and it has a kind of nineteenth-century stereo effect, namely being able to make it sound as though bells were ringing outside the church. I can see why the tourists flock there, for it is magnificent and should not be missed.

As we left Passau we were overtaken by a huge barge from Bulgaria with lorries neatly parked on the deck. I asked Captain Frolich, or Captain Non-stop as we had now affectionately named him because he had dredged up this new English phrase which he used frequently, what the purpose of these lorry transports was. It seemed that the Austrians had become annoyed with the number of heavy lorries thundering across their country towards Germany, and had imposed a quota system for lorry movements. The Bulgarians had decided that the best thing for them to do was to build four barges able to transport forty-nine lorries at a time from Bulgaria to Passau. Once safely in Germany, they were unloaded and driven off to their various destinations. It was interesting to see the normal roles being reversed and some more work being put back on to the rivers. The drivers seemed to like it as they sat on the deck by their lorries,

201

playing cards as they sped along on their four-day trip.

As we passed the junction of the Inn and the Danube there was a marked change in the colour of the water. The Inn must have a lot of chalk in it somewhere upstream because its water was a kind of milky white whereas the Danube is much darker. We did not have far to go until we came to the border post at Obernzell, where we stopped and dutifully showed our papers, to the Germans first, and then to the Austrians posted in a tiny shack directly opposite on the other side of the river. I was surprised to learn that Austria had not yet joined the Common Market.

An Austrian friend had told me that in Germany they say, 'The situation is serious but not disastrous,' and in Austria, 'The situation is disastrous but not serious.' I rather looked forward to a little humour after the slightly sombre time that we had had in Germany.

CHAPTER THIRTEEN

Passau to Vienna

Our progress down the Danube took on a stately demeanour with Captain Non-stop guiding the boat skilfully through all hazards. He had the most extraordinary eyesight and could pick out the nationality and size of on-coming barges before I could even see them. He would wave only to the captains of barges from Austria and Germany and never to anyone from the Eastern Bloc countries. Ray and I made up for this by waving at just about everyone and getting a satisfactory response. The waving was a relief, staving off boredom as we travelled though mile after mile of densely wooded valleys which swept right down to the water's edge. From time to time there was the odd strip of field with some old lady dressed as one would imagine a peasant to be dressed, with faded headscarf and canvas apron. Here and there were orchards but for the most part it was Heidi country.

On the northern shore, the tourist department has come up with a marvellous arrangement for cycling holidays. Because the Danube has been tamed to some extent with dams and locks, the towpath or access road is flat, perfect for the middle-aged cyclist. Moreover, spaced along the Danube are guesthouses run not by hotel chains as they would be anywhere else, but by individual families who take a pride in having the same people back year after year.

We stopped one night at the pontoon at Schlögen, which is so called because the giant bend in the river looks like a giant sling. The family that owned a big old guesthouse there had festooned it with the heads of wild boar and whatever else they had hunted over the years. They had taken hunting trips to Hungary by river all through the Cold War – the division of Europe seemed to make very little difference to them or, probably, to the wild boar. I should have thought that once you had one savage head up on the wall, licking its chops and staring at you in the dining room while you ate, you would have found it quite sufficient, but the family who decorated this place seemed to have a passion for these sombre beasts. I found out afterwards that they also bred wild boar in a small farm hidden in the forests – explaining why there were so many different dishes made from the indigestible meat on their menu.

The Captain slipped back to his wife in Linz and we stayed for a day in Schlögen to try to repair the battery charger which was causing us a good deal of difficulty. There is nothing so important, except of course a sound hull, as the electricity supply on a boat. Our generator was working beautifully but the batteries were not recharging properly. The batteries were the backbone of the system: we had something called an inverter to convert our 24-volt DC current to 220 volts AC, vital for all the small modern appliances that we have come to rely on so heavily, such as electric razors and battery chargers for radios. We found in the local town, thanks to the Captain's information, a battery dealer who could supply us with a suitably powerful battery charger. He was a young man but insisted on talking to me like some Austrian count in an operetta. Constantly calling me, 'My dear Mr Goodwin', he gave me the giggles, causing me to lose my way completely with his strictures about ampere hours and overheating. The gentleman he sent to fix the battery charger into the boat thought it was very funny and though he could not speak English imitated his boss, 'My dear Mr Goodwin', perfectly and we all laughed a good deal about this incredibly stilted phrase.

The Captain arrived early the next morning with a plastic bag of lunch which he started to prepare as soon as he set foot on board. This time it was his favourite goulash again –

paprika, beef, thinly sliced onions, kümmel (a German liqueur, flavoured with aniseed and cumin) and masses of garlic – which the Captain adored. I did not mind it but Ray is one of those unfortunates who are made quite sick by such a dish, so we had an awkward moment when Ray finally indicated that he could not eat any of the Captain's masterpiece. During the morning we had passed through some of the most beautiful countryside on the Danube and had stopped at another pontoon to enjoy our goulash. All these pontoons are owned and operated by the DDSG, which stands for Donau-Dampschiffarhtgesellschaft, a semi-governmental company which takes care of all the official Austrian trading on the Danube. The pontoons are made up of substantial tanks, held away from the shore by massive pine logs, allowing deep-draught vessels to come alongside and also coping with the considerable rise and fall in the river level during the year.

The Captain and I could converse now in some strange language that we both seemed to understand which was hardly German nor was it English, but he was able to give an impression of life on the Danube and of how it is changing, with bigger and faster craft owned by huge national concerns replacing those owned by individuals or family companies, making the whole river more impersonal. The boat people on the river had a fierce independence and were not very happy with the imposition of national rules on their lives; they would make the most complicated plans to avoid stopping in countries like Rumania, where even the shortest stop would mean hours of paper checking and handing out Kent Long Filter cigarettes, which have become a currency in Rumania. I am told that if you want anything done, there is a tariff measured in packs and cartons of this particular brand. Apparently the only people who actually smoke these cigarettes are prostitutes, who do so for effect.

That evening we pulled into a village called Neuhaus Oberzell which had been completely rebuilt higher up the hill on which it stood, after the valley was flooded when the dams were built to harness the wild river in the 1960s. This village is on a very pretty bend in the river and we went alongside the quay on one side of the village square. As we tied up, a brisk white-haired gentleman hurried up to the boat and asked what we were doing on the 'Blue Danube' and without waiting for an answer asked why we had a large antenna on the boat. I explained that we had a short-wave radio and his eyes lit up: he was a short-wave enthusiast. He at once invited us to go and see his 'shack' in the top of his house. We accepted, but there was a certain amount of discussion about the time and he was obviously strictly controlled by his wife. We agreed to go to his house at eight; he said we would recognize it by the antennae on the roof. He promised to get in touch with England for us, which seemed a pretty dotty idea.

The world of the amateur radio ham is truly quite unlike anything else. The greatest television sketch ever to be filmed on the subject is without question Tony Hancock's piece, 'The Radio Ham', which follows the inanities of their contacts. Radio hams spend a great deal of money on their equipment and their conversations are confined to what the weather is like in their part of the world, what type of equipment they have and what they are transmitting on at that particular moment. Finding the shack was not difficult: in a village with no more than ten houses the one with aerials festooning the roof was fairly easy to identify.

Our new friend introduced himself with, 'The handle is Herman.' His callsign, which we were to hear many times that evening, was Ocean Echo Five Delta India Lima. He made good his promise and called up a contact in Truro in Cornwall called Tony and I had to suppress a fit of giggles when they went into their 'What's the weather like?' routine; 'Yes, it is raining here also.' His shack was the top of the house, squashed out of his wife's way, in a small room which was completely stuffed with equipment of all sorts. He was able to bounce signals off satellites and do all manner of things that a simple phone call would do at a tiny fraction of the cost. The appeal lay, he said, in never knowing with whom you would be exchanging news. Herman was a doctor and had been in charge of public health for the whole of upper Austria until his retirement some years ago. Since then he had devoted his considerable energies to his hobby and to making radio commercials for public health on Austrian radio. He called up another couple of his mates and then confided that the Kings of Jordan and Spain were keen radio hams. I asked, tongue-in-cheek, whether there was a private network for royalty, but he replied very seriously that there was not. He signed off to his callers with, 'See you down the log,' the log being a list of all the contacts he had made and their addresses so that he could send one of the postcards he had had printed of himself at his transmitter with his call-sign emblazoned over his head. Herman would also wish people 73s which apparently meant 'kind regards' in CB talk; 99 means 'shut up'. As we left he kindly gave us a bag of organically grown apples.

As we entered Linz, we heard the sound of two girls' voices echoing off the sides of the valley. When we rounded a bend we saw the girls sitting by the edge of the Danube and yodelling their throats dry, practising for some competition they were entering. Fascinated, we asked the Captain to stop and we moored and went to quiz these Danubian Lorelei about what they were up to. They were an enterprising pair. Gertie worked in a butcher's and Gaby was a secretary in an office; they had taken up yodelling as a way to earn a little extra. They concentrated their efforts on the hotel boats that came up and down the river and earned commissions from the boat companies to yodel a welcome to the passengers as they joined their ships in Linz. They told me that they were particularly popular with the Russian tourists. I do not suppose there is a great deal of yodelling in the Soviet Union.

The next morning dawned grey and grim. The autumn was setting in and it was distinctly chilly when the Captain stepped aboard after spending a night at home with his wife. This time his plastic bag contained the ingredients for his special Matrosen Fleisch. We passed by the huge steel works, grim and threatening in the watery sun that was just managing to struggle through low polluted clouds. We had gone about an hour down river when I saw a sign pointing to Mauthausen Concentration Camp. We tied up on a pontoon and got out the bikes and pedalled up the long hill to that infamous place. I had never seen a concentration camp before and none of the films that I had seen had prepared me for the horror of seeing one of these places, so starkly preserved by the Soviets during the period that this part of Austria was under their occupation. I will not go into details of the pathetic cupboards of photographs that the Italian, Spanish and Russian families had fixed to the walls or describe the images that will be with me for the rest of my life. Man's inhumanity to his fellow man has never before been so vividly demonstrated to me.

The Captain had his meal prepared when we got back to the boat but he quite understood when Ray and I said that we did not have an appetite. Ray steered and I sat on the deck thinking about what I had seen. The Captain finished his meal and said simply that this was the kind of thing that happened if you allowed dictators to take over. It was very hard to tell what he was thinking as he gazed down the river, which was getting misty as the autumn evening drew in. That night we stopped in a district called the Wachau and I took Ray and the Captain out for a meal of the local fish called zander which is a kind of pike and particularly good. There was a need for a little cheer after our morning in that terrible place.

After a couple of hours next morning we came to a village called Grein which was famous for being the place where passengers descending the Danube, before the blasting away of rocks that caused whirlpools, used to disembark with all their valuables from the boats in which they were travelling, leaving the experienced pilots to make their way through the boiling maelstrom whilst they rode horses along the bank. They would get on again in St Nikola about two kilometres downstream. The town hall in Grein is small and the old granary built on to it is the smallest working theatre in Austria with 163 seats. Mimi Kessler told me about these seats which one could buy at the beginning of the season with a key. You locked the seat up when you left and when you wanted to use the seat you had to unlock it and let the flap drop. She also told me that this had been the only theatre in Europe that had a lavatory actually in the auditorium. When the theatre was built everything was ready except the door to the loo, so they just put up a curtain. This proved to be a great success with the occupants because they were able to watch the show through the join in the curtain without curtailing their activities. Mimi was a witty charming woman who came from Grein and had spent the war as a cook for the landed gentry in Bathampton and Yorkshire. She spoke of her terror and confusion when she had first arrived as a refugee in 1938 and had been asked to cook pancakes which she did not have the slightest idea how to make. I am sure that she always had the wit to charm her way out of any such predicament.

The next morning I made a stupid mistake by deciding to take the boat up the river a way to see how well we went into the current. Captain Non-stop had been held up and I thought that while we were waiting for him to reach us on the bus from Linz we would try this little experiment. All was well as I went upstream but as soon as I turned to come back the current got hold of the dinghy which was trailing astern and flipped it over. Luckily, this time, we had followed the first rule with outboard motors and had tied it on, but the oars and the life belt and anything that was loose in the dinghy fell out and either drifted off or sank. It took Ray and me some time to right the dinghy with the crane and when we reached the pontoon again, the Captain, who had arrived and seen what had happened, rightly summed up the incident with, '100 per cent *Absolut Catastroph'*.

A pretty innkeeper's daughter (they do exist) came up to the boat and talked to us about her childhood playing on the beaches they used to have on that stretch when the water level dropped in the summer before they built the dams and locks. Her family had been pilots for generations when it had been obligatory to take on a pilot to negotiate the *Wirbel*, or whirlpool. The girl, whose name was Maria, told hair-raising stories that her father and uncle had told her of the disasters they had seen and of how it had been impossible to reach the survivors on a stricken barge once it had struck a rock in the whirl. Her mother's inn was full of pictures of these marine disasters and of the floods that they used to have which had reached the second floor of their pub.

Maria told me that a very interesting man who had been a doctor in these parts lived nearby. All his life he had dreamed of owning a romantic castle overlooking the site of the whirlpool. I decided to bicycle there and so I told Ray and the Captain that I would meet them in St Nikola, where the pilots had been dropped in former times. I arrived at what appeared from the road to be the ruin of a small castle but, as I drew closer, I saw that it had been carefully restored. I rang the long rope bell-pull and waited for what seemed like an age until the door opened, letting a great shaft of sunlight through and giving the old man who appeared a white halo as the sun shone on his hair. The good doctor was well over ninety and seemed to be held together by an incredibly ancient and stiffened pair of long lederhosen. He was delighted to show me round his domain and proudly pointed out the plaques of the families that had lived there; these came to an abrupt halt in the 1400s – and then there was his. The castle had been a ruin from the time of the Crusades until this dauntless doctor had taken it on when he retired. He had turned it into a tranquil place and told me that the air from the pine trees was what had allowed him to live so long. At one stage in the nineteenth century an English aristocrat had bought the castle and hung a huge Union Jack from the remains of the tower – the old man showed me a watercolour of it. He also showed me a huge collection of pictures of the whirlpool and the various ways the ancients used to negotiate it. This apparently useless intelligence was to become extremely useful within the hour. I admired this dauntless old man's garden, breathed the air deeply on his instructions, bade him farewell and shot off down the hill on my bike.

The boat was in the appointed place but one look at the faces of the ship's company made me realize that there had been a '100 per cent *Absolut Catastroph*'. I was greeted with, 'The prop's fallen off,' and it was soon apparent that there was absolutely no way that we were going to be able to retrieve it in what must be the deepest part of the Danube; we were now in a fjord-like valley where the bottom must be at least two hundred feet below the surface. I heaved my bike on board and as I did so I had an idea. The print at the castle had shown how the ancient boatmen on the Danube had steered their craft with long oars called sweeps. I realized that we had the means to make something similar. I had bought a bit of ¾-inch chipboard which I had made into a table for eating on deck and I thought that if we cut that in half and bolted the bits on to the two long scaffold poles we carried, we could make two excellent sweeps.

Even though we were in a remote place, a small group of incredulous spectators had gathered to watch our progress. We had no problems constructing our sweeps but we knew that if, before nightfall, we were to reach the shipyard about fifteen kilometres downstream where Captain Non-stop had his contacts, we had better be on our way. When Ray and the Captain had brought the barge into the shore without the aid of the engine, they had crash-landed, which meant

211

that we were firmly stuck. It would have been easy to get off had the engine been working, but alas, with no propeller, it was useless, so we had to get everything absolutely ready, untie the barge and wait for another vessel to come past, creating sufficient swell to lift the barge for a split second while we pushed her off. The first ship that came by was a German barge that saw we were in difficulties and considerately slowed down to pass which was no good. We had to wait for a large Bulgarian lorry carrier to come past at full speed – this was enough to dislodge us. While we were waiting we had dried out the outboard after its morning dunking and got that going, so with Ray and me pushing as hard as we could to get the *Leo* out into the stream, the Captain revved up the outboard on the dinghy at the stern. In a few moments we were facing upstream in a seven-mile-an-hour current and slipping slowly backwards. We had to turn the boat as soon as possible, otherwise we would be pushed sideways into the bank and then we would be really stuck.

The Captain had tied the dinghy on to the port side of the stern of the *Leo* and so we had to turn round to port in as tight a circle as we could, otherwise the current would catch us and push us down sideways. Ray and I stuck our oars in and pulled with all our strength, while the Captain opened the throttle on the outboard: we started, very slowly, to turn. I was quite sure that we would not get round but somehow our efforts succeeded and the bows just missed the bank on the far side. We were round and heading downstream. Our progress was fair when the current ran straight but when there were eddies and other unpredictable currents the outboard alone was not strong enough so we had to lean on our sweeps and pull as hard as we could. Fortunately, the Captain really knew his river and was able to give us warning when these places were coming up. It took us five hours to get to the shipyard at Ybbs and we arrived just as it was getting dark. We tied up with some difficulty and the Captain sprang

212

ashore and went to talk to his friends in the shipyard to see whether they had a nut that would fit and a crane to lift us out of the water. While he did this, I called up London on the short-wave radio to see whether the office had been able to get a nut made which I had ordered after our last mishap a month before in Germany. They had ordered it but it had not been made, which was not cheering news, and I hoped that the Captain had had better luck.

That night Ray and I were too tired to eat but I felt honour bound to cook something for the Captain who was a regular eater and so I cooked that reliable standby, spaghetti *carbonara*. As the Captain munched through his pasta and bacon, he told me that we had to be ready at seven in the morning when the foreman had promised to pull the *Leo* from the water on a trolley and then assess the problem. This yard was an official establishment and therefore was not really allowed to do outside jobs, but luckily they were not too busy and the Captain indicated that a small present to the workers' canteen would open all doors.

We were on the trolley, which was marked with a stick in the water, at seven sharp on the most perfect morning in probably the world's most scenic shipyard. With no delay at all the *Leo* was slowly winched on to dry land and the foreman engineer came to measure the naked shaft so that he could look for a nut. He took one look at the problem, ran his thread gauge over the shaft and briskly said he would have to make a nut and it would take an hour, would that be all right? An older man, who was a deaf mute, asked, using sign language, for the spare propeller that Ray was holding and carried it off to the workshop. Just then a hooter went and everyone disappeared for breakfast while we were taken to the manager's office by one of the men and offered a glass of chilled vodka. I felt it was churlish to refuse, but the effect of one vodka on an empty stomach, followed swiftly by another, is lethal and I found myself in a daze for most of the morning. Ray, rather wisely, had managed to avoid this

213

toast; the Captain had not, but it appeared not to make the slightest difference to his progress.

By ten o'clock a new nut had been made, a hole drilled through the shaft, and a pin placed through the nut and the shaft so that the propeller can now never come off again. The dents on the propeller had been removed and we had said our farewells to these amazingly kind people. I hope our tiny contribution went some way towards a jolly good party in their canteen: they deserved it. Within half an hour we were at the next lock where our papers were looked at very carefully because I had taken a photograph of the shipyard from the side of the lock. It turned out that there was a building at the end of the lock which housed a turbine for electrical power and I suppose the lock-keeper thought he was guarding the national security secrets of Austria.

The weather in those early October days was beautiful and the leaves were turning in the proper fashion. Our next stop was the vast monastery at Melk which was a great resting place for travellers to Vienna. Built on a great bluff above the Danube it had been conveniently placed a day's journey by carriage or boat from the city. Almost all the historical luminaries had been entertained there by the monks, ever since the thirteenth century. When one particular Pope had visited he had found himself unable to pay for the food for his vast retinue, so had donated instead the relics of some Christian who had died in Rome. I suppose you made sure you never left home without a relic or two that you could give away, just in case you got a bit short of cash. In this case, no one knew who the martyr had been, so they all came to the very practical decision of calling him Frederich. Napoleon had come uninvited, and Marie Antoinette had visited, to name but two who had stayed in the great state rooms. The library is very fine indeed and looks out over the Danube valley so that I am sure that scholars can very easily be distracted by the view. This part of the Danube is particularly imposing for the river traveller, and was one of the reasons that I had been drawn to make the journey, because I had read a nineteenth-century writer called Planché who had described its beauty when he made a trip on the Danube in the early 1840s.

The blue church of Dürnstein was our next beacon. High above it was the fortress where Richard Coeur de Lion had been incarcerated and where as legend would have it he heard the minstrel Blondel singing his favourite hit. The local schoolmaster told me the Austrian version of this story which was not quite what I remember being told about our heroic adventurer king in the home classroom that Mrs Shuttleworth ran in Bombay. It appeared that the co-leader of the Crusade had been an Austrian duke, Leopold V, who had led the attack at the Battle of Acre and, having heroically stormed the fortress, had hoisted his national flag to the battlements. Richard, as official leader of the Crusade, had objected, and the two warriors had fallen out. The Austrian had returned to his homeland, muttering revenge, and Richard had returned to England. He had been shipwrecked and found himself travelling up the Danube in disguise. He must have had a predilection for young blond friends, or Blondels as they are known in that part of the world, because he had lent one of them his gloves to cut a dash when he went shopping. The boy's gloves had been recognized and Richard incarcerated; in due course the Austrian had become thirty-five tons of silver richer. Looking up at the fortress, I realized that to hear anyone singing by the river from the castle required an embroidery of the possible.

After the pretty town of Dürnstein the valley opens out into a plain stretching down to our goal, Vienna. We had one last stop to make at the boatyard where, after we had been to Vienna, I proposed to lay up the *Leo* for the winter. Captain Non-stop brought us to the shipyard at Korneuburg where some large ships were being built and some of the pre-war paddlewheelers were being repaired. One of the modern ships that was being finished was going out on its

215

trials the next day and the Captain, who had a cousin who worked in the yard, got permission for us to look over the ship, which was being built for the Russians. It was a 5000-ton refrigerator ship which had more massed technology on it than anything else I have ever seen. Everything had at least two, if not three, back-up systems and everything was automatic. The Russian captain was an extremely jolly man who merrily complained that it was 'too much automatic'. I asked him if he was automatic himself, which made him laugh, and since it was his birthday we all went off to celebrate in his office. We postponed our triumphal entry into Vienna until the next day; I *think* he said it was his birthday!

It is said that all great cities have their knees in the water, but Vienna merely dips an extended toe into the Danube. Like London in August, the city reminded me of an empire that had gone on vacation. Captain Non-stop brought us to a berth that belongs to the DDSG, situated just under the Sweden Bridge on the canal that runs parallel to the Danube itself. Unlike any of the other cities we had stopped in, the towpaths were not particularly popular with the inhabitants. For some reason the usual crowd of lovers and dog walkers were far fewer, so it was a surprise when I heard a voice with an authentic British nautical ring about it calling out 'Ahoy, *Leontyne*.' The owner and his companion came on board and they told me that their passion in life was a four-masted sailing schooner, of which they were part owners and which they kept on the north-east coast of England. They were an engaging couple, and, having heard a number of their nautical adventures, I asked them what they did for a living. To my great surprise, the gentleman told me that his name was Professor Müller, Principal of the famed Vienna Conservatory of Music and his friend, a pretty, slim girl, was the Professor of Guitar. They invited me to visit the Conservatory and we arranged to meet in a couple of days.

The Sweden Bridge lies just off the area popularly called the 'Bermuda Triangle', because so many people have disappeared into the narrow streets and alleys. Being Austrian, though the streets are narrow they are spotlessly clean, except of course near the McDonald's emporium where those horrible cardboard chip-holders always lay littered. Ray and I visited some of the famous cafés and had a game or two of billiards but the *Zeitgeist* was not with us.

The visit we made to the sewers where Carol Reed had made his masterpiece, *The Third Man*, was more in keeping with the Vienna I had imagined. When I had started in the film business as a tea boy and then third assistant director, I had worked for a man who had been an assistant director on *The Third Man*. He taught me all I know of how to handle irascible artistes. One of the things he told me that stuck in my mind was that it was always very wise to wear clothes of the same colour and type each day on a film because it reassured both the crew and rage-blinded creators. Just as a red rag enrages a bull, quiet colours soothe.

The entrance to the main sewers built in Emperor Franz Josef's day was just off the main road in Karls platz. The men who showed me round, like many people who do slightly unsocial jobs, were very pleased to see me. The smell in the main chambers took a little getting used to, but as we descended through the neat granite masonry the air cleared and we found ourselves in the main sewer. This is in fact the River Wien, which is almost entirely covered in. It was here and in the passages leading off it that Carol Reed had created his nail-biting chase at the end of *The Third Man*. As a film maker, I was amazed by how he had managed to make so very few locations seem like a vast labyrinth. As we climbed up to the street level again the man who was guiding me, dressed in white overalls and huge leather thigh boots, showed me how some strange secret society had got into the sluice room by cutting through the lock on a steel door and had then conducted some sort of Black Mass amongst the sewage. The wax from their candles was still visible in little worm casts on the floor.

I went to see the nautical musician at the Conservatory of Music and had a marvellous introduction to the world of music as it flourishes in Vienna. The Conservatory has students from all over the world and the numbers from each country fluctuate with the progress of music in those countries. When he started, the Chinese had sent many students but now they have so many trained musicians in China that the students come from other countries. The Principal said he could never understand how students from the Far East, raised on a music with quite a different tonality, could learn Viennese and Western music so rapidly. He told me his greatest challenge was training a group of Arab musicians whom the King of Jordan had sent to Vienna to be trained in Western music. After the first year he said that he had very nearly given up. His staff were in despair but they persevered and at the end of five years they were all playing well enough to give performances to the public. He confided to me that he was far more expert in stellar navigation than he was in counterpoint, which impressed me.

After riding round Vienna on a tram and a bike, eating well and dining at *Heurigers*, those strange Viennese institutions spread round the edge of the city which sell their own wine and a lot of schnitzels, I decided to ask the Captain to leave his home in Linz and take us up to Korneuburg. Ray and I were eager to get on our way again and so were happy to see our friend the Captain walking along the towpath with his Burberry neatly folded over his arm and carrying a plastic bag containing a delicious cake from Mrs Frolich.

The trip to Korneuburg should have been simple but the Captain said the current would be exceptionally strong, for it had rained in the mountains some days before and the surge had just hit the river at Vienna. As usual, he was right, and we took two hours to struggle up the canal as far as the Danube; once we were in the main river we made absolutely no progress at all. We watched as some Eastern Bloc ships went past but the Captain said there was no way they would help us. Then, as luck would have it, he saw a friend of his churning up the river in a huge barge laden with coal. He called him up and we were soon alongside a 2500-horsepower monster of a barge from Germany which hefted us to Korneuburg in an hour.

We tied up and said goodbye to the Captain, then made our final arrangements for the boats, which were going to be lifted out of the water for the winter and put in a shed, for the river freezes in these parts. Packed and drained, I left the *Leo*, heroine of so many adventures, alone. I had left our flag flying on the stern and, as I walked up the gangway in the setting sun, I watched it flutter in farewell.